A CASE FOR
CHRISTIANITY:

Establishing a Foundation for Faith

WILLIAM GOLSON JR.

Order this book online at www.trafford.com
or email orders@trafford.com

Most Trafford titles are also available at major online book retailers.

Print information available on the last page.

ISBN: 978-1-4907-7949-2 (sc)
ISBN: 978-1-4907-7948-5 (e)

Trafford rev. 12/13/2016

Trafford
PUBLISHING® www.trafford.com
North America & international
toll-free: 1 888 232 4444 (USA & Canada)
fax: 812 355 4082

CONTENTS

CONTENTS

ACKNOWLEDGEMENTS

This book is written on the sunset of more than 28 years as Senior Pastor. As I reflect upon retirement, I have had the privilege to pastor and preach to the membership of True Light Baptist Church. During this time as I have prayerfully attempted to address their needs, God has faithfully spoken into my life as well. I have grown in wisdom and benefited through the opportunity to address relevant issues biblically. My life has been influenced, I have been sharpened, by the circumstances, situations, and opportunities of those who have allowed me to share in resolution of their challenges.

My deepest thanks go out to those who have allowed me to be a part of providing counsel in their lives. I am thankful to have been a part of their journey. *"Ointment and perfume delight the heart, and the sweetness of a man's friend gives delight by hearty counsel."* (Proverbs 27:9)

Thanks to my staff (Sable Golson, Bonne Tootle, and Jeanie Draper) have always diligently ensured that I have the time to do what is needful and are always willing to do whatever it takes to assist me in hearing the voice of God. Thanks to Flo Callaway for her assistance in proofing the manuscript.

I dedicate this work to those who invested early in the planting of True Light Church; and to my dear mother, Maldoshia Golson, who went home to be with the Lord (June 2015). Whatever I have become is a result of having come from good seed, and having been nurtured along the way by a true example of a saintly mother. Her wisdom, example of righteous living, and love for the Lord have been and will continue to be my guide and strength. My parents, William and Maldoshia, were married for over 68 years and gave their full support for my ministry.

In addition, I dedicate it to my wife, Melvia Jo who has been by my side in the planting and growth of this church and has helped me to understand the meaning of being a husband and father. It has been my privilege to be her pastor. Thanks to my children Melody and William III, who have endured, in the arena of raising them to adulthood, my often-misguided attempts at parenting, but who despite my mistakes, by God's grace have grown to be godly individuals of whom I proudly boast to be my children. *"Behold, children are a heritage from the Lord, the fruit of the womb is a reward. Like arrows in the hand of a warrior, so are the children of one's youth. Happy is the man who has his quiver full of them; they shall not be ashamed, but shall speak with their enemies in the gate"* (Psalm 127:3-5). Thank you.

INTRODUCTION

Becoming a Christian is easy, in the sense that there is no application to be completed, no rigorous training program, no requirement to matriculate through a series of classes, or any certifications to obtain. However, in the simplicity of becoming a Christian: acknowledging sin, confessing, asking for forgiveness, accepting the substitutionary death of Jesus Christ, being born again, beginning to live a life of faith, and growing in the knowledge of the Word of God; we often fail to understand some of the basics. Therefore, our faith foundation is not as solid as it should or could be.

It is comparable to being an auto mechanic, carpenter, or other profession and not knowing about the tools of your trade. The believer's basic tool, guide for living, is the Bible; the Word of God. It is the foundation of our faith and therefore we should understand some of the basics about it: how it was written, the spiritual personalities it speaks of, what kind of life it calls us to, and the confidence we can have in a commitment to live according to its precepts.

Within the context of these pages, we will attempt to make *A Case for Christianity*; that is, to present evidence that will hopefully affirm your belief and strengthen your faith as a Christian. We will not argue nor cloud our case with arguments for or against other religious persuasions; we will simply present evidence as to justify being a Christian.

Additionally, we will attempt to promote an understanding of who we are and what we have in Christ Jesus. The life we live as Christians often conflicts with what the Bible says we should be about. When faced with the reality that we often fall short, often fail to live up to biblical expectations; we can either become discouraged, quit, give up, bear the heavy weight of guilt, or we can realize that we are not perfect.

Satan, who is the Devil, Beelzebub, the accuser of the brethren, the prince of demons would have us believe that we have never been anything, are now nothing, and will never be anything. He would have us believe that we have this extremely fragile relationship with a God who just waits for us to do one thing wrong, and then separates Himself, and takes back the blessing of His salvation. The Devil would have us believe that a God who is Holy, just, and righteous will have nothing to do with those who are any less, especially those who say they believe but who don't live up to it. He would tell us that the church is full of hypocrites, those who claim to be one thing but whose actions are totally contrary. Many have believed that lie and have turned away from the church. Many have believed that lie and have turned away from God believing that He could not love them. Many have believed that lie and separated themselves from spiritual things for fear they might be labelled a hypocrite. But the truth is that we are in the process of trying to get our flesh to line up with our spirit. Trying to bring this practice of life into alignment with our position in Jesus Christ. Some of us just about have it, others do not.

The church is not perfect, never has been and never will be. If you are looking for a perfect church you have two choices; either find one which has no membership, no people, or pack your bag and schedule a one-day trip to heaven. The church is made up of people, and as long as there are people in the church there will be problems, there will be those who sin.

Although we are challenged to live a life of holiness we cannot in this life achieve it in its fullness. Even the best of us from time to time will stumble and fall. It is my hope that you will find comfort and security in knowing that your life is eternally secure in Christ.

What is presented here is a simplified, and concise, explanation of some deep doctrine, some deep spiritual concepts. There are hundreds, if not thousands, of books written on each topic that is discussed: The Bible, God, Jesus, the Holy Spirit, sin and others. My goal is to give a general observation, summarize the crucial issues, and try to provide the best answers. More details could be added, but it is my belief that filling out the details would not change the answers; it would only make them stronger.

These topics may generate more questions than answers and my hope is that it will drive you to further study. To aid you in your quest, and for further study, I direct you to a helpful Christian website *www.gotquestions.org*.

CHAPTER 1

"WHAT ABOUT THE BIBLE"

"All Scripture is given by inspiration of God, and is profitable for doctrine, for reproof, for correction, for instruction in righteousness." (2 Timothy 3:16)

As we begin the development of our case, we want to start by laying a foundation for faith. What we are called to believe and will come to believe must first be established as to its veracity, meaning its honesty, truth, and reliability. The Bible is the basis, the standard, and the foundation by which we claim a faith in God: His work of and in creation and in the lives of those He created; the incarnation, meaning God coming to reveal Himself in the flesh in the person of our Lord and Savior Jesus Christ, and the new birth experience whereby we stake our claim to eternal life, and the resurrection and hope of eternal life. With all this at stake, we must believe and know that the Bible is the very Word of God. It reveals the essence of His character, the outflow of His mind, and His expression of love and destiny for all creation.

Therefore, we come to the bar of justice, before the court of public opinion, to make *A Case for Christianity,* to present the case for our faith in God and salvation through His Son, Jesus Christ. We accept the challenge as it is declared in 1 Peter 3:15, *". . . sanctify the Lord God in your hearts, and always be ready to give a defense to everyone who asks you a reason for the hope that is in you, with meekness and fear."*

In our society, and particularly for our current younger generation, the lines between right and wrong, between truth and error, between Christian influence and cultural accommodation are becoming increasingly blurred. For some there are no absolute standards, no moral laws, and no spiritual values by which we are to be governed. Every person may decide for himself or herself what is right. When it comes to talking about God, right and wrong, good and evil, and salvation all is relative.

Although God allows us the freedom to decide how we will live our lives, with that kind of relative thinking, morality becomes a non-issue, and almost every kind of deviant behaviour becomes acceptable. However, one cannot live out relativism because all of life ultimately consists of one true-false judgement after another. Eventually, one must commit oneself to something as true and its opposite as false.[1] Therefore, without a real and true word from heaven, a standard from God, people are lost in a sea of human opinion and moral weakness.[2]

Having said that, let us begin with the consideration of the Bible, the Word of God. What do we know of the Bible?

IT IS THE SELF-PROCLAIMED INSPIRED WORD OF GOD

"All scripture is given by inspiration of God . . ."
(2 Timothy 3:16)

Direct communication from God is called revelation. The revelation is of typically of two types: *general* and *special*. The physical evidence of God as seen in His creation is usually called *general* revelation. The revelation given us in His Word, the Bible, is generally called *special* revelation. God and His Word are inextricably tied, meaning, we cannot talk of one apart from the other.

In the text before us, the apostle Paul declares, *"All scripture."* To which Scripture is Paul referring? Although various epistles, meaning letters written by apostles-the major part by Paul, were in circulation, the New Testament was not yet written. Therefore, Paul was referring to the Old Testament and the personal testimony that Timothy, the letter's recipient, had of the Gospel, which would later become the New Testament. The New Testament resided in the hearts of men long before it took the form of being codified, meaning assembled, as a book. Regarding the Word of God residing in the heart, Paul says of the believers at Corinth in 2 Corinthians 3:2, *"You are our epistle written in our hearts, known and read by all men; clearly you are an epistle of Christ, ministered by us, written not with ink but by the Spirit of the living God, not on tablets of stone but on tablets of flesh, that is, of the heart."*

Furthermore, Paul admonishes Timothy that "a*ll scripture is given by inspiration of God."* By inspiration, we mean that the Holy Spirit exerted His supernatural influence upon the writers of the Bible. In the context of the Scriptures, the word "inspiration" simply means "God-breathed."

J. W. McGarvey, a famous Restoration preacher of a century ago, compared inspiration to driving a well-trained horse. You pull the rope to the left or right as you see the horse needs guidance; you slow him down when he goes too fast; you speed him up when he goes too slow, but most of the time you just let him go on his way. Your hand is always on the rope and the horse always feels the pressure of your hand. As the authors of the Bible wrote, they felt the pressure of God's direction, His inspiration, on their lives.

The process of inspiration is:

- Not all of God and none of man-this would-be dictation.
- Neither was it all of man and none of God-this would-be humanism.
- Nor was it 50 percent of God and 50 percent of man-then errors of major magnitude would be inescapable.

But the real picture is that God used men in their total activity, and yet He worked upon them powerfully, being 100 percent in control. God's hand was upon the writers of Scripture to lead them in certain directions while at the same time allowing them to utilize their personalities and write within the context of their cultural settings. The result was that the Bibles authors wrote as no ordinary people wrote, but *"as they were moved by the Holy Spirit"* (2 Peter 1:21). Like most spiritual truth, this view involves mystery. But it is a wonderful mystery, and it has given us an inerrant Bible.[3]

IT HAS A SELF-PROCLAIMED PURPOSE

Here's a pop quiz: Which of the following statements do not originate in the Bible?

- Cleanliness is next to godliness.
- God helps those who help themselves.
- Confession is good for the soul.
- We are as prone to sin as sparks fly upward.
- Money is the root of all-evil.
- Honesty is the best policy.

Though we may agree with these statements; each is true or at least partially true, and although they may be valuable and reflect some element of biblical wisdom, none of them is in the Bible. Often lacking in our biblical understanding, we have learned to treat man's opinions with as much respect as the Bible.

However, the Bible clearly guides us on how to receive and live life to the fullest, both now and for all eternity. In its purpose, Paul declares of the scriptures that it *"is profitable for doctrine, for reproof, for correction, for instruction in righteousness: . . ."* (2 Timothy 3:16c-e)

Doctrine or *Teaching* focuses on the Bible as giving us instruction to live life. Now this assumes that we come to the Bible as learners, because only learners can be taught. This instruction or teaching isn't just about heavenly things, but it's about practical things like being a good spouse, being a good parent, loaning out money, starting a business, and so forth. Therefore, the Bible provides us with the **CONTENT** of our faith.

Reproof or *Rebuking* sounds kind of harsh, but really, it just means confronting our wrong ideas about life. All of us carry around misconceptions and distortions about God, about ourselves, and about life that needs to be changed. For instance, if we measure success in life by how much money a person has, but the Bible measures success by a person's faithfulness to God, then our criteria for success has been rebuked, and we need to change our definition to conform to God's definition. Therefore, the Bible provides us with **CONVICTION** when we go astray from the faith.

Correction is similar to rebuking, but it focuses in on behaviour instead of beliefs. This assumes that all of us lose our way in life sometimes, that we can easily wander off the course God has for us and end up roaming around in circles. The Bible corrects us when it gets us back on track in life, when it shows us where we are and how to get back on course with where God wants us to go. Therefore, the Bible provides us with guidance as to how we might **CORRECT** our mistakes.

Instruction in righteousness focuses on the Bible's role in helping us live the kind of lives that please God. This assumes that a life of integrity does not come naturally to us, that we need help to live the kind of life of integrity we want to live. The Bible trains us to do that which we could not do on our own when it comes to a life of integrity. [4] Therefore, the Bible provides us with principles to apply to life so that we might develop Christ-like **CHARACTER**. The Bible's purpose is to provide:

- The **CONTENT** of our faith.
- **CONVICTION** when we go astray from the faith.
- Guidance as to how we might **CORRECT** our mistakes.
- The development of our Christ-like **CHARACTER**.

IT HAS MANY AUTHORS BUT IS ONE BOOK

"Knowing this first, that no prophecy of Scripture is of any private interpretation, for prophecy never came by the will of man, but holy men of God spoke as they were moved by the Holy Spirit." (2 Peter 1:20-21)

When God spoke to people in early times, it was an oral (or verbal) special revelation. As far as we know, there was no writing until after the Flood. God's oral revelation, however, was just as special and inspired as His latter written words. The words themselves are truly Gods words inspired by the Holy Spirit.

Moses was the first writing prophet. A prophet in Israel was not just a highly spiritual man. A prophet was a man called of God to receive revelation from Him (Numbers 12:2-8). The prophets word was so much God's Word that it was as if the prophet had eaten a scroll from heaven and had given it out orally to the people (Ezekiel 2:7-3:3). The word spoken was God's word. The same must be said of the words wrote. Much, if not most, of the Old Testament was spoken first and written afterwards. This is true of the New Testament as well.

The Bible is a compilation of 66 different books written by 40 different authors from three different continents in three different languages: Hebrew, Latin, and Greek, and written over a period of 1,500 years. There are 66 books of the Bible, 39 in the Old Testament and 27 in the New Testament. The Old Testament is written primarily in Hebrew, with a little Aramaic, and the New Testament is written exclusively in Greek. These books form what is known as the canon "the rule of law" and contain different literary forms or genres, such as history, poetry, humor, prophecy, romance, letters, biographies, songs, journals, advice, laws and stories. The authors were kings, fishermen, priests, government officials, farmers, shepherds, and doctors. Yet, within each of the 66 books, we read an incredible unity of themes from Genesis through Revelation, progressively revealing God's plan to restore

His creation. [5] Each of these authors in their own way presents a unified portrait of God's plans and purposes in our world.

For 40 authors, with such varied backgrounds, to write on so many subjects, over a period of approximately 1,500 years, in absolute harmony, is a mathematical impossibility. It could not happen! Then how do we account for the Bible? The only adequate explanation is[6] found in 2 Peter 1:20-21, *"Knowing this first, that no prophecy of Scripture is of any private interpretation, for prophecy never came by the will of man, but holy men of God spoke as they were moved by the Holy Spirit."*

Holy men of God were *moved*, or inspired, *by the Holy Ghost*. God used the prophets and controlled them, but He did not violate their distinctive personalities, writing styles, and cultural settings to speak or write in his own way the very words of God without error in fact, doctrine, or judgements.

We believe, as did Jesus and the apostles, that the 39 canonical books of the Old Testament are the inspired Word of God. The 27 books that make up the New Testament were written over a 50-year span, and they deal with Jesus Christ's birth, life, death, and resurrection, the beginning of the Christian church, and instruction about how to live as a follower of Jesus Christ.

There were other writings, but those books were omitted for a variety of reasons. Some of which are designated the *Lost Books of the Bible,* or the Apocrypha-included in Roman Catholic Bibles-are not quoted in the New Testament. They were not lost. They just were not accepted as part of the canon, the book of the Bible. Why weren't they accepted?

1. Because they were not recognized by early believers as being inspired by God.
2. The 27 books, which form the NT canon, all contain quotes from almost all thirty-nine OT canonical books, but not once from the Apocrypha. [7]
3. Jesus and the apostles manifested their approval of the 39 OT books in that there are significant references and

quotes. The others were not. The Apocryphal books are not.

The Bible, as we now know it, is a divine library with many human authors, but we must always remember the Bible is a single volume, one book, written by one Author, the Holy Spirit. The book has one great theme, redemption of sinners; and one great historical thread, God's saving dealings with fallen humanity.

****

What people say about us often does not matter. It may be untrue, unkind, irrelevant, and prejudiced. What we say and believe about ourselves matters more in that it works on us and in us to shape our personal and worldview. However, what we believe about the Bible and what it says about us matters most!

What we believe about the Bible is no small matter because it contains the very essence of life itself. We must get it right! We cannot say that we do not care; we cannot be indifferent; we must believe something about this book. Paul said to Timothy, *"from childhood you have known the Holy Scriptures, which are able to make you wise for salvation through faith which is in Christ Jesus."* (2 Timothy 3:15)

The Bible can in like manner make us wise for salvation through faith in Christ Jesus. The Bible informs us:

- All have sinned. (Romans 3:23, Romans 5:12)
- The wages of sin is death. (Romans 6:23)
- God demonstrated is love towards us. (Romans 5:8)
- We must confess. (Romans 10:9, 10, 13)
- God so loved. (John 3:16)

The bible tells us that salvation is through Jesus Christ.

- If you are cold, let it WARM you.
- If you are asleep, let it WAKE you.

- If you are a backslider, let it WARN you.
- If you are defiled, let it WASH you.
- If you are disobedient, let it WHIP you.
- If you are uncertain, let it WITNESS to you.
- If you are unsaved, let it WIN you.[8]

Each of us at some time or another must wrestle with the question of why are we here. Where are we going? Is this all there is? What is the basis for our living and conduct in this life? If we believe in some kind of a hereafter, the decisions we make about life have eternal consequences. In other words, what we are after here will affect our hereafter. What standard we use has eternal consequences.

It is important to know what we believe. *I know whom I have believed and am persuaded that He is able to keep what I have committed to Him until that Day* (2 Timothy 1:12). It's important to know what we believe, because what we believe will affect the way we live our lives.

REFLECTIONS AND MEDITATIONS

1. What is the basis of your moral code?
2. The Bible is not man's book; it is the Word of God.
3. Are you willing and open to allow the Word of God to fulfil its purpose in you?

CHAPTER 2

"WHAT ABOUT THE BIBLE: EXHIBIT A"

". . . that you may know the certainty of those things
in which you were instructed." (Luke 1:4)

We do not here merely intend to prove the Bible from the Bible. Although, that should be, and is sufficient for those of us who believe, but we ought to be aware of other evidences as well. Our faith is not a blind leap into the dark but a sensible step into the light. Although Christianity is founded based on faith, it must be logical and real with a "provable," quality to it. And as any courtroom observer knows, proof requires evidence. Genuine faith believes because of powerful evidence, not inadequate evidence. That evidence exists.[9] As we attempt to prove the veracity of the Bible, meaning its honesty, truth, and reliability, we bring before the court the testimonies of physical evidence, eyewitnesses, and prophecy.

THE TESTIMONY OF PHYSICAL EVIDENCE

The first question in the mind of a sceptic is not whether the Bible is theologically inspired, but whether the Bible is historically reliable.[10] Can we trust the Bible? Is Scripture sufficiently trustworthy to stake our lives upon it? We begin with the testimony of the . . .

OLD TESTAMENT

We do not have the original documents, called autographs, of the Old Testament, as for instance we do the Declaration of Independence. The original writings were recorded on papyrus (an early version of paper), vellum (typically some form of animal skin), clay, and lastly paper. Over the centuries, either natural decay or intentional destruction has resulted in us having only fragments and copies of copies of copies. How then can we know that we have the real deal?

First, the scribes, these copyists, were so dedicated to their task that they meticulously tried to assure that all copies were exact duplicates of the originals. The scribes were highly skilled men who apprenticed under expert transcribers of the text.

The scribes had very strict laws for copying. They would count every word of the book they were working on in the original, identify the middle word, then the middle letter. Say a book had 7,000 words. Say the middle word was God. The middle letter of God, of course, would be "o". They would write all this down. Then they'd begin copying letter for letter, and word for word. When they were done, they would go back and count the words-7,000, good. They would then find the middle word, and middle letter. If the middle letter, say, was G instead of "o" the copy that took weeks to complete was destroyed and a new copy was begun.[11] The result was a remarkably faithful transmission of the text, not perfect as it would be today with a copy machine, but a remarkably faithful transmission.

Experts have determined that there are 14,000 manuscripts and fragments of the Old Testament. If you lay all of them side by side, you'll find one variation every 1,580 words, and 99% are spelling variations![12]

Second, recent discovery has validated the copies. In the summer of 1947, a young Arabian boy lost track of one of his goats. The region was Qumran, in the Middle East, the hillsides overlooking the Dead Sea. When his goats wandered into a cave, the boy chased it. He threw a rock into the cave hoping to scare the goat out and heard pottery breaking. Upon investigation, he found several clay pots containing scrolls.

Eventually the scrolls found their way into the hands of some Israeli scholars. They looked in the caves and found over 20 caves full of scrolls. Old Testament Scripture was found in various forms: clay writings, papyri, leather scrolls, which contained portions of the canon in part and in the case of Isaiah in total.

Since then other caves have yielded additional Old Testament manuscripts and related Jewish material. Thousands of fragments are still being patiently pieced together and studied. All the Old Testament books except one have been found in the caves. The book of Esther has not yet been identified. Some books, such as Psalms, Deuteronomy, and Isaiah, are represented in many copies. Others, such as Chronicles, are present only in fragments. The greatest scroll is Isaiah, preserved completely and in good condition. What does this find tell us? The Dead Sea Scrolls are remarkably like the Hebrew bible from which our modern translations occur. This twentieth century find proves that those who copied the Hebrew Bible through all the years back to the second century before Christ did an extremely careful job. It establishes that our Hebrew Bible in nearly its present form was used by the Jews 200 years before Christ. [13] There were some minor misspellings and variant words, but there was no substantial difference between the ancient scrolls and the words you and I have in our Bibles today.[14]

The early Church Fathers believed that any seeming contradictions that appear in the Bible are due to lack of knowledge of the times and customs of the people or to minor errors of copying. But the original autographs themselves are what we call *inerrant*, or without error.

NEW TESTAMENT

When it comes to the New Testament, the physical evidence for the acceptance of the Bible is overwhelming. There are 24,000 copies of the New Testament: 5,300 in Greek dating to within twenty-five years or so of the actual writings, 10,000 in Latin, and 9,300 in other languages. Lay them side by side and you'll find less than one variation in 1,000 words. The variations are from a scribe copying a word wrong or inverting a letter. [15] The number of manuscripts in support of the reliability of the New Testament text (and their chronological proximity to the original writings) is far beyond anything else known in human literature. Therefore, we can be assured that what we are holding is God's Word.

The sheer magnitude of Old and New Testament Scripture original documents, serves to authenticate the Bible to be more than just a book. The testimony of physical evidence is that the Bible is the very Word of God.

THE TESTIMONY OF EYEWITNESSES

Several years ago, during a homicide trial in Nassau County in the state of New York, the prosecution was examining their witness on the stand. In his testimony, the witness stated that he saw the victim lying on the ground, obviously dead. When the prosecution had finished, the defense lawyer rose to his feet intent on undermining the credibility of the witness and conducted the following cross-examination: "Sir, are you a doctor?" "No," replied the witness. "Well, are you a paramedic?" "No, I'm not," the witness stated. "Have you ever gone to medical school?" "Never," was the answer. "Then tell me, sir, how do you know that the victim was indeed dead?" "Well," responded the witness, "I went to his funeral." In every crime scene investigation, it's hard to beat the value of eyewitnesses. [16]

In any court of law, as well as in all things spiritual, *"Every matter must be established by the testimony of two or three witnesses"* (2 Corinthians 13:1, NIV). The most compelling evidences of the veracity of the Bible, the most significant fulfilment of prophecy is the resurrection. The resurrection is the thread that runs throughout Scripture. All Christianity hinges on the Resurrection. Can we find three witnesses to testify to the resurrection and therefore, the authenticity of the Bible?

The gospel writer Luke opens his gospel with the following declaration to his friend Theopholis, *"Inasmuch as many have taken in hand to set in order a narrative of those things which have been fulfilled among us, just as those who from the beginning were eyewitnesses and ministers of the word delivered them to us, it seemed good to me also, having had perfect understanding of all things from the very first, to write to you an orderly account, most excellent Theophilus, that you may know the certainty of those things in which you were instructed."* (Luke 1:1-4).

The apostle Peter affirms to his fellow believers, *"For we did not follow cunningly devised fables when we made known to you the power and coming of our Lord Jesus Christ, but were eyewitnesses of His majesty."* (2 Pet 1:16)

The apostle John includes not only visual, but also physical validation, of his relationship with Jesus, *"That which was from the beginning, which we have heard, which we have seen with our eyes, which we have looked upon, and our hands have handled, of the Word of life."* (1 John 1:1)

The apostle Paul gives the most convincing evidence for believing in the resurrection of Christ *declaring that after being resurrected; "He was seen by Cephas, then by the twelve. After that He was seen by over five hundred brethren at once, of whom the greater part remain to the present, but some have fallen asleep. After that He was seen by James, then by all the apostles. Then last of all He was seen by me also, as by one born out of due time."* (1 Corinthians 15:5-8)

In a court of law, when we have two or three witnesses whose stories are all presented exactly alike, we begin to suspect that they have gotten together ahead of time to rehearse their accounts. We strongly suspect conspiracy. However, if each person tells the story from his or her own perspective, each adding different and sometimes additional details, and yet not contradicting the testimony of the others, we can more easily assume we are getting a genuine story. The fact of Jesus resurrection is attested to by not one, two, or even three witnesses, but by more than 500. Their testimonies may not exactly agree. However, the variance in their testimonies are not necessarily contradictions in the history. On the contrary, these minor discrepancies provide powerful evidence that the accounts are true. [17]

The gospel writers had a testimony of witness, the apostles had a testimony, people down through the ages have had a testimony, if we have been converted we have a testimony-not an eyewitness testimony, but we have the testimony of a changed life.

THE TESTIMONY OF PROPHECY

> *"For I delivered to you first of all that which I also received: that Christ died for our sins according to the Scriptures, and that He was buried, and that He rose again the third day according to the Scriptures."* (1 Corinthians 15:3-4)

The apostle Paul declares to the believers at Corinth that what he has delivered, was what he received, was based on Scripture. In his testimony, he declares that Jesus life, death, and resurrection were according to the Scriptures.

No book in history has dared to predict the future to the degree the Bible has, without being proven wrong. No other historical work makes the predictions that the Bible does. Someone has calculated that the Bible contains 1,817 individual predictions, concerning 737 separate subjects, found in 8,352 verses, that's 27% of the 31,124 verses found in the Bible! [18]

Statisticians say that if you or I were to list 100 things predicting what a person was going to be like, it would take two hundred billion earths, as full of people as ours, to come up with a person who fully fulfilled those prophesies. Old Testament Scripture records not just 100 prophesies about Jesus, it records 300 that were fulfilled in His first coming alone. By man's standards,

100 prophesies are impossible—much less three times that amount. Someone else has calculated that if we were to cover the state of Texas with quarters, two feet deep, mark the back of 1 of them with an X. Fly a man in and drop him anywhere you want in the state, blindfold him, and ask him to find that quarter with the X first try! That's the same chance of just eight of the Bible's prophecies being fulfilled by coincidence![19]

When we study Old Testament prophesy and see how true and accurate and detailed it is, there is no doubt God is the author. God is the author and He doesn't lie. In the Old Testament, the prophets described everything about Jesus, including the fact that He would come as our Savior and King. Every prophecy was published at least 500 years before Christ was born.

- Micah 5:2 predicted that the Messiah would be born in Bethlehem.
- Isaiah 40:3 predicted He would be preceded by a messenger (John the Baptist)
- Zechariah 9:9 predicted He would ride triumphantly into Jerusalem on a colt.
- Psalm 41:9 predicted He would be betrayed by a friend.
- Zechariah 11:12 predicted He would be betrayed for 30 pieces of silver.
- Psalm 22:16-17 predicted He would be crucified 600 years before it was invented.
- Isaiah 53:12 predicted that the Messiah would be crucified with thieves.
- Psalm 16:10 predicted that He would be raised from the dead

The most compelling evidence of the veracity of the Bible, the most significant fulfilment of prophecy is the resurrection. The resurrection is the thread that runs throughout Scripture. All Christianity hinges on the Resurrection. The apostles pointed to the empty tomb and fulfilled prophecy as the major evidences confirming Christ's claims. [20] Without the resurrection, the scarlet thread of redemption from Genesis to Revelation makes no sense.

The apostle Paul would say it this way in 1 Corinthians 15:14, 17-19), "... *if Christ is not risen, then our preaching is empty and your faith is also empty. . . And if Christ is not risen, your faith is futile; you are still in your sins! Then also those who have fallen asleep in Christ have perished. If in this life only we have hope in Christ, we are of all men the most pitiable.*"

Scientist Henry Morris put it this way, "The bodily resurrection of Jesus Christ from the dead is the crowning proof of Christianity. If the resurrection did not take place, then Christianity is a false religion. If it did take place, then Christ is God and the Christian faith is absolute truth."[21] The testimony of prophecy informs us that the Bible is the historical record of the Word of God.

****

A preacher by the name of Vance Havner once cleverly and humorously remarked, "Many people say the Bible is a myth, but they're myth-taken, myth-guided, and myth-erable." [22]

Satan has declared that the bible is nothing but a myth and works hard to discredit it. He knows that what it says is Truth. He knows that God told the prophets to tell about the coming Messiah. And they did. And they did it accurately. So, since Satan can't discredit the prophesies, all he can do is cast doubt on the text itself. Over the centuries, he has tried to belittle it, burn it, and bury it.

- He says the Bible is full of mistakes.
- He says it was written by men with an agenda.
- He says it was written by men other than who the Bible identifies as the authors.

However, Satan's attacks on Scripture don't hold water; there is too much evidence to the contrary.

Luke wrote to his friend Theophilus that he might know the truth, the certainty of what he had been told, and that he might have a firm foundation on which to believe. When we understand:

- there are thousands of fragments that when pieced together validate the Old Testament—we have a firm foundation.
- there are thousands of original documents of the New Testament—we have a firm foundation.
- the level and complexity of prophecy that has been fulfilled—we have a firm foundation.

This evidence demands a verdict! No other can be found, or determined, other than the Word of God, the Bible is true, and Jesus Christ is the Son of God.

Yes, there is proof in the fact that we have physical evidence; yes, there is proof in that we have the testimony of eyewitnesses; and yes, there is proof in that Old Testament prophecy and predictions have all been fulfilled. But the greatest proof is in my personal testimony, and your personal testimony, that because of Jesus we have been changed.

The Bible is more than a book. It is salvation to the sinner, sanctification to the saint, it is sufficient to the suffering, and satisfying to the scholar. Its teachings are so deep the scholar can swim in it for a lifetime without ever touching bottom, yet so simple; a child can approach it for a drink, without fear of drowning! I love its depth, but the greatest truth, the greatest proof, I have ever learned is this: Jesus loves me this I know, for the Bible tells me so! [23]

REFLECTIONS AND MEDITATIONS

1. The evidence demands a verdict that the Bible is the Word of God.
2. What would be the personal testimony that you could share as to the Bible being the Word of God?

CHAPTER 3

"IN THE BEGINNING GOD"

"In the beginning God created the heavens and the earth. (Genesis 1:1)

In the previous chapter, we argued for the veracity of the Bible, because unless the Bible is truth, then the opening statement of Genesis 1:1 that establishes God as our creator is a lie.

What are the two main beliefs about our origins? One is atheism and evolution, and the other is the Bible's account of creation. What are these two different beliefs?

1. If we believe in the theory of evolution, that life began billions of years ago, by a cosmic accident called The Big Bang:
   - We are only complex animals with no ultimate purpose or meaning in life.
   - Our final destiny is to become worm-food, rotting in the grave.

2. If we believe in the Biblical account of creation:
   - We are a special and unique creation of God and life has great purpose.
   - Our final destiny is to live forever with God in the paradise of Heaven.[24]

The Genesis account of creation is, strictly speaking, not history, for the events of creation happened at some point before history began. Nor is it science, it is not the result of investigation or some systematized experiment. It is not myth; it is not a traditional story focusing on the deeds of some divine personality to explain some natural phenomenon. If Genesis is not history, or science, or myth, what is it? The Biblical account of creation is revelation. It is the Word of God; given by God, to inform, comfort, and assure His children who are willing to read and believe. It is the revelation of His ability to create something from nothing that gives us hope during our darkness, amid our chaos and confusion.

WHY DO WE NEED TO CONSIDER
THE ORIGIN OF THE EARTH?

Today there is much controversy over the teaching of creation versus evolution in our public schools, even in some of our seminaries. Those who support the evolutionary view that man evolved from monkey or some other lower life form is an attempt to portray their view as scientific while they portray the Biblical account of creation as just some kind of religious folklore. On this basis, they seek to bar the biblical account of the creation, and all other religious influence, from discussion in our schools.

The simple fact is that both those who hold to the theory of evolution and those who believe in special creation must come to their respective positions by an act of faith. Obviously, there were no eyewitnesses. No one was there in the beginning and therefore no human being has an actual account. The Christian believes in divine creation because he believes the Bible as the Word of God, ultimately an act of faith, but as was shared in the previous chapter, not without physical evidence, eyewitnesses, and prophetic evidence. In like manner, one who believes in evolution would expound scientific evidence, but ultimately both must also come to a position by an act of faith.

Since both the creationist and the evolutionist come to their positions by faith, we might say that evolution and creation are both religions. Therefore, this issue is not just about science, but faith. Many have used evolution as an excuse not to have faith in God. God? Just a myth. Sin? No big deal. If Genesis is true, who sets the rules? God does. If Genesis can be discredited, who then sets the rules? We do. If we believe Genesis to be a myth, then we are not accountable to anyone but ourselves. We can make up our own rules. Nothing is right or wrong: kill, lie, steal, and cheat. It is all part of the survival of the fittest. Love has no meaning.[25]

On the other hand, if we believe that God created the universe with moral laws as well as physical laws to govern it, then our approach to life will be dramatically different. We will feel obligated to learn God's moral laws and learning them, we will seek to obey them.

In our society, we have seen an eroding of values; life is worth little and is taken for the simplest reason. Humanity has come up with a justification for everything: homosexuality, lesbianism, child molestation, murder, rape, and host of other things. As a society, we are rewriting biblical standards, which have made this country the great country that it is, to conform to our own sick little mentality, to our own self-serving desires. The bible is surely true when it declares in, Proverbs 14:12, *"There is a way that seems right to a man, but its end is the way of death."* Our world right now is filled with death. Each day we pick up the paper, turn on the TV, listen to the radio, or other media outlet; it cries to us of death: drive-by shootings, abortions, wars, murders, aids, and drug overdoses.

The problem lies with our understanding, our view, of who created this world, and to whom we belong. Satan has brought before us the lie that we created ourselves, that we are some kind of a cosmological accident. Satan has ever so cleverly eroded Christianity in our school systems that every concept of God is taboo. Almost everything is allowable in our schools except for the bible and prayer: condoms, Halloween, Satanic clubs, Harry Potter, and mysticism to mention a few.

They teach alternative life styles:

- They teach supposed safe sex, which in actuality is safe fornication.
- They teach humanism, that man is creator and controller of his destiny.
- They allow Satanism and every dark side of life to be glorified.
- They teach that plants and animals, dogs and cats, have as much worth and as much value as human beings, when in actuality nothing compares to man who was created in the image and likeness of God.

I have a dog, Shadow, I treat him kindly, I respect his position as an animal, I love him, but he has no rights, he is just a dog, and a dumb dog at that. That is not just my perspective; that's bible. When we don't acknowledge our awesome creation as humans, we place ourselves on the level of dogs and cats. And we wonder why our children have no respect for life, for authority, for themselves. Genesis 1:27 declares of humanity, *"God created man in His own image; in the image of God He created him; male and female He created them."* Our society has no concept of God as creator and therefore our society have set out to make up its own rules.

Let no one dismiss the controversy between evolution and creationism as only a political or theological debate. We need to consider the origin of the earth because our children are being taught religion in school, whether they want to call it that or not.

THE EVIDENCE OF CREATION

"In the beginning God created the heavens and the earth..." (vs. 1)

Modern science has provided us with many interesting theories about the origin of our universe. A popular theory of recent years is, often referred to as the "Big Bang" theory. According to this theory, several billion years ago a tremendous explosion sent light and matter hurling across the vast reaches of space. From all this matter, heavenly bodies were formed. Of course, the theory does not answer the fundamental question of where the ingredients for the big bang came from.

We will go into this more in our next chapter, but for the moment, the unity, and order of the creation show that there must be some form of intelligence behind its existence. The concept that such order came about by an accident defies human imagination as well as human intelligence. When one looks at automobiles that have just crashed head-on at fifty miles an hour, do we see in that "Big Bang," a vivid portrayal of harmony and order? On the contrary, all the elements of creation interact so harmoniously that the thinking person is irresistibly driven to the conclusion that behind all of creation is a majestic intelligent person. Business leaders take the following quote very seriously: "Quality is never an accident; it is always the result of intelligent effort." Why, then, do so many scientists refuse to apply this truth to the realm of origins?[26]

The universe did not come into existence by chance or by explosion. The universe was made to fit together and to have meaning. The Christian can be certain that when he argues from the uniqueness, the complexity of the design to the designer that he is exhibiting a clear head. Chance, as an explanation of the origin of the universe, is an invention of the mind.

Psalm 19:14a (NIV), speaks of general revelation, in that, if nothing else the heavens themselves declare God as the designer, *"The heavens declare the glory of God; the skies proclaim the work of His hands. Day after day they pour forth speech; night after night they display knowledge. There is no speech or language where their voice is not heard. Their voice goes out into all the earth, their words to the ends of the world."*

The message of the sky is plain and continuous, though it is silent. The message of the sky is unbroken. Each day passes it on to the next, and again the sun sweeps the horizon to horizon with its blazing proclamation of Gods glory. Likewise, each night picks up the message of the night before and displays God's handiwork in millions of twinkling points of night. Silent as it is, the message reaches the whole world. The sky uses sign language, not spoken words; but it gets its message across. The author and cause of this great work is God.

Hebrews 11:3 (KJV) declares, *"Through faith we understand that the worlds were framed by the word of God, so that things which are seen are not made of things which do appear."* The old preachers used to say that God stepped out on nothingness, reached back through nowhere until he got somewhere and found something, and then he brought something from somewhere back through nowhere until he got somewhere, and took something and hung it on nothing and said, "Let there be!" Yes, the very complexity of our earth, or our human body, is evidence of divine design. Psalm 139:14 declares to God, *"I will praise You, for I am fearfully and wonderfully made."*

GOD IS STILL CREATING.

"The earth was without form, and void; and darkness was on the face of the deep. And the Spirit of God was hovering over the face of the waters." (vs. 2)

As we consider the starting point of creation, the Scriptures tell us that all was in chaos. The earth as we now know it:

- was without form and void.
- was full of confusion and emptiness.
- was shapeless.
- was useless.
- was without inhabitants, without ornaments.

In its primitive state, the earth was without form and void. It was just a great blob of material encircled by a mass of clouds. No light was shone upon the earth; darkness was everywhere. The deep is the term used for the ocean, and in this early stage, water covered all the face of the earth. However, the Spirit of God was moving, hovering, brooding over the unfinished earth, and some changes were to be made. God was in the process of bringing earth to a condition appropriate as a dwelling place for humanity.

Some of us can reflect upon when, like the earth, our lives were in chaos.

- We were without order; existing in a state of spiritual ruin.
- We were without life; being dead in trespasses and sins.
- We were without light; shrouded in darkness; walking, perhaps, in the fire of our own wisdom, but devoid of that true light which is from heaven.

For some of us, our lives are still chaos. There seems to be nothing but darkness in the answer to every circumstance of our lives. No matter what we do there seems to be no light. Everything is just a mass of confusion, there seems to be no order, there is no purpose, and there seems to be no plan. However, know that the Spirit of God is moving, the Spirit of God is hovering, the Spirit of God is brooding over our circumstance ready to take our chaos and confusion and bring them forth as a great creation to God's glory.

God is still creating, not new heavens, or new earths, but new beings, spiritual beings. Second Corinthians 5:17 says, *"Therefore, if anyone is in Christ, he is a new creation; old things have passed away; behold, all things have become new."*

Whether we are better or worse, God still claims us as His. As the Spirit of God brooded over chaos, so does God's Holy Spirit hover over fallen souls, waiting for the commanding word to declare, "Let there be" which would introduce light, order, into our life. God wants to make us a new creation today!

****

In the early days of the automobile, a man's Model-T Ford stalled in the middle of the road. He couldn't get it started no matter how hard he cranked nor how much he tried to advance the spark or adjust things under the hood. Just then, a chauffeured limousine pulled up behind him, and a wiry, energetic man stepped out from the back seat and offered his assistance. After tinkering for a few moments, the stranger said, "Now try it!" Immediately the engine leaped to life. The well-dressed individual then identified himself as Henry Ford. "I designed and built these cars," he said, "so I know what to do when something goes wrong."

God made the world and everything in it, including you and me. What difference does it, make? What does this have to do with our daily living? God created us to live peacefully and prosper. If our life is in a mess, that was not God's intention for us, and only the creator, the divine designer, can fix what is wrong. God, as our creator knows how to "fix" us when our lives are broken by sin.[27]

Each of us has a part to play in the creation of the mess in our world, in our homes, and in our personal lives. Each of us must be personally responsible for our understanding of who and whose we are and how we fit into the magnificent plan of God's creation.

As we go into the world, we come face-to-face daily - with others who feel as though the words *"everything is formless and void, and darkness is surrounding the deep"* describes their lives. They feel as if there is no hope. If this happens to be true in your life, there is good news for you today. Because, it is exactly at this point that God begins to work. What an incredible gift - knowing, that in our time of darkness - when we need Him the most, God is right there, waiting for us to turn to Him, waiting to create new life in an otherwise empty world. He is always there waiting and wanting to create something extra-ordinary in your life.

REFLECTIONS AND MEDITATIONS

1. Is your life in chaos?
2. God, as our creator knows how to "fix" lives are broken by sin.

CHAPTER 4

"IN THE BEGINNING GOD: EXHIBIT A"

"In the beginning God created the heavens and the earth." (Genesis 1:1)

The story is told of a little boy who was drawing a picture. His kindergarten teacher asked him what he was drawing. He said he was drawing a picture of God. She said, "But no one knows what God looks like." He answered, "They will when I'm done."

No one knows what God looks like, yet the opening words of Genesis 1:1 assume that there is a God. There is no argument, there is no justification, and there are no presented proofs. It simply states *"in the beginning God."* Having previously reasoned and concluded that the Bible is truth that is all that we, as believers, need. However, is there any further evidence?

There is no way that we can consider all the proposed arguments regarding God. The goal here is to give a general observation, summarize the crucial issues, and try to provide the best answers.

LOGICAL ARGUMENTS

In the previous chapter, we discovered about God as creator; Scripture informed us that apart from any other evidence, there is general or natural revelation of God as seen in the creation. General revelation is God's communication of Himself to all persons at all times and in all places.[28] The complexity of the universe and the human body, the order and existence of the laws of the universe, all beg for the existence of an intelligent designer. What other arguments might we pursue in affirming God's existence to be true? In addition to the biblical arguments for God's existence, there are logical arguments.

First, we consider the logical argument for God's existence called the **COSMOLOGICAL ARGUMENT**. The cosmological argument derives its title from observing the world around us (the cosmos). The idea is that we assume the existence of God from what we see in the world: [29] In the common experience of everyday life when we observe that something exists, we are called to consider and ask how it came to be.

Let us take a simple example: trees. All trees began to exist at some point (for they have not always existed). Each tree had its beginning in a seed (the "cause" of the tree.) However, every seed had its beginning ("cause") in another tree. We cannot have an infinite series of tree-seed-tree-seed—it cannot go on forever. All series have two endings actually—at the end and at the beginning (if you do not see why this is true, try to imagine a one ended stick!). Everything has a cause. It was caused by something that was caused by something that was caused by something, etc. There must be something that caused everything to come into existence. Ultimately, there must be something "un-caused" to cause everything else to come into existence. That "un-caused" cause is God. There must be something at some time that started it all, a first cause. The universe was caused by an eternal, non-contingent being. That "un-caused" cause is God. [30]

Second, we consider the **TELEOLOGICAL ARGUMENT**. The word teleology comes from telos, which means "purpose" or "goal." The idea is that it takes a "purposer" to have purpose, and so where we see things obviously intended for a purpose, something had to have caused it for a reason. The teleological argument states that since the universe displays such an amazing design, there must have been a divine Designer.

One of the most popular forms of this argument is the Watchmaker analogy, first used by William Paley. It says that if you are walking in a field and you find a stone, you can assume that natural processes formed it. If you find a pocket watch, however, you can assume that an intelligent designer made it. You make this assumption because the watch exhibits intelligent design. It has a spring to give it motion, gears and wheels to transmit the motion, the gears are made of brass so they will not rust, the spring is made of steel (which is flexible enough for springs), and the front cover is made of glass so you can see the face. It is obvious that thought and purpose went into the watch. Trillions of years of natural processes could not have created it. Its complexity, purpose, and design point to an intelligent designer. Then Paley pointed to the universe and the life within it. It is much bigger and more complex than a watch and it is unlikely that natural processes and chance could produce such a complex and purposeful universe. In other words, design implies a designer.

A third argument is known as the **MORAL ARGUMENT.** Every culture throughout history has had some form of law. All people recognize some moral code (that some things are right, and some things are wrong). Every time we argue over right and wrong, we appeal to a higher law that we assume everyone is aware of, holds to, and is not free to change arbitrarily. Right and wrong imply a higher standard or law, and law requires a lawgiver. Because the Moral Law transcends humanity, this universal law requires a universal lawgiver. This, we argue is God Himself. Where did this sense of right and wrong come from if not from a holy God? [31]

You may remember the story of Jeffery Dahmers who killed 17 men, and ate them! In a statement during his imprisonment (before he was put to death) said, "If man is a product of blind chance and there is no God and there is no meaning to life then who are you to tell me what is right and wrong?" Yet, every one of us would agree that Dahmers' acts were very evil. We all have a sense of right and wrong, don't we? We may not always agree on what is right or wrong, but we all believe that there are things that are right or wrong. So, where does that come if not from a Holy God?

The cosmological argument shows that God must be eternal, uncaused, and very powerful if He created the entire universe. The teleological argument shows us that God is highly intelligent if He designed such a complicated and functional universe. It also shows us that He is purposeful and pays a lot of attention to details. Finally, the moral argument shows us that God is a moral being. He created morality and He Himself is completely good. It also shows us that He wants us to be good.

BIBLICAL ARGUMENTS

As we have seen, there are a number of logical arguments for the existence of God. None of which can prove conclusively the existence of God, but show based on various arguments that God is. That an infinite intelligent being exists who has shaped, fashioned, and called into being all of creation.

When it comes to the matter of God, there are people in our world who look at what we believe and say they do not believe God exists (atheists), or they say they cannot know if God exists (agnostics). Both groups basically say, "We've not seen enough evidence to believe God exists."

The story is told of one such individual who supposedly confronted an old Quaker and taunted him: "Have you ever seen God? Have you ever felt God? Have you ever smelled God? Ha! And you say you have a God!" Show me, where is the evidence? Where is the proof? The Quaker thought for a couple of moments and then replied, "Hast thou ever seen thy brains? Hast thou ever felt thy brains? Hast thou ever smelled thy brains? Ha! And thou sayest thou hast brains!" Now, I do not if that story is true or not . . . but Scripture agrees with that old Quaker. In Psalm 53:1, David declares, *"The fool has said in his heart, there is no God."* Why would such a person be a fool? Well, because, there is more than enough evidence to believe God exists.[32]

The Bible does not try to prove the existence of God. However, the Bible does give some strong pointers in the direction that belief in God is reasonable. The Bible says that we must accept by faith the fact that God exists. Hebrews 11:3, 6 declares that a belief in God superintends, or overrides, a relationship with Him. *"By faith we understand that the worlds were framed by the word of God, so that the things which are seen were not made of things which are visible . . . But without faith it is impossible to please Him, for he who comes to God must believe that He is, and that He is a rewarder of those who diligently seek Him."*

If God so desired, He could simply appear and prove to the whole world that He exists. But if He did that, there would be no need for faith. However, John 20:29 tells us that blessed are those who believe apart from physical evidence, *"Jesus said to him, "Thomas, because you have seen Me, you have believed. Blessed are those who have not seen and yet have believed."* [33]

In several places, we read and learn about God from nature. The Bible states in Psalm 19:1-4, *"The heavens declare the glory of God; and the firmament shows His handiwork. Day unto day utters speech, and night unto night reveals knowledge. There is no speech nor language where their voice is not heard. Their line has gone out through all the earth, and their words to the end of the world. In them He has set a tabernacle for the sun."* Looking at the stars, understanding the vastness of the universe, observing the wonders of nature, seeing the beauty of a sunset—these things point to a Creator God.

If these were not enough, there is also evidence of God in our own hearts. Ecclesiastes 3:11 tells us, *"He has put eternity in their hearts."* Deep within us is the recognition that there is something beyond this life and someone beyond this world. We can deny this knowledge intellectually, but God's presence all around us and in us is still obvious.

Despite this, the Bible warns that some will still deny God's existence: *"The fool has said in his heart, "There is no God"* (Psalm 14:1). Since the clear majority of people throughout history, in all cultures, in all civilizations, and on all continents, believe in the existence of some kind of God, there must be something (or someone) causing this belief.

Despite these arguments, the Bible tells us that people will reject the clear and undeniable knowledge of God and believe a lie instead. Romans 1:25 declares of humanity, they *". . . exchanged the truth of God for the lie, and worshiped and served the creature rather than the Creator, who is blessed forever. Amen."*

A BELIEF IN GOD BRINGS RESPONSIBILITY

It does not seem to have occurred to any of the writers of either the Old or the New Testament to attempt to prove or to argue for the existence of God. Everywhere and at all times, it is a fact taken for granted. The Scriptures simply declare *"In the beginning God."*

Each of us at some time or another must wrestle with the question of why are we here. Where are we going? Is this all there is? What is the basis for my living and conduct in this life? It's important to know what we believe, because what we believe will affect the way we live our lives. Some people claim to reject God's existence because it is "not scientific" or "because there is no proof." The true reason is that once they admit that there is a God, they also must realize that they are responsible to God and in need of forgiveness from Him. If God exists, then we are accountable to Him for our actions and the decisions we make about life have eternal consequences. The basis of godlessness is to ignore God. And at the heart of godlessness is ignoring nature's clear declaration that there is a God and you will one day have to deal with Him. Romans 1:20 proclaims that people are without excuse for not believing in God: *"For since the creation of the world His invisible attributes are clearly seen, being understood by the things that are made, even His eternal power and Godhead, so that they are without excuse."* [34]

If God exists, the Bible informs us of our condition, our opportunity, and our responsibility:

- Our condition—all have sinned. (Romans 3:23, (Romans 5:12)
- Our condition—the wages of sin is death. (Romans 6:23)
- Our opportunity—God demonstrates His love towards us. (Romans 5:8)
- Our opportunity—God so loved. (John 3:16)
- Our responsibility—we must confess. (Romans 10:9, 10, 13)

If God does not exist, then we can do whatever we want without having to worry about God judging us. That is why many of those who deny the existence of God cling strongly to the theory of naturalistic evolution—it gives them an alternative to believing in a Creator God. God exists and ultimately everyone knows that He exists. The very fact that some attempt so aggressively to disprove His existence is in fact an argument for His existence. [35]

****

A little boy who was talking to his dad, who was an atheist-one who continually affirmed that he did not believe in God--at dinner. The little body said, "Dad, do you think God knows that we don't believe in Him?" That was one of those questions where to answer yes or no would affirm the existence of God. It is easier to prove the existence of something than it is to prove the non-existence of something. [36]

For example, someone may claim that a red eagle exists and someone else may claim that red eagles do not exist. The former only needs to find a single red eagle to prove his claim. However, the latter must comb the entire universe and literally be in every place at once to ensure he has not missed a red eagle somewhere and at some time, which is impossible to do. Therefore, intellectually honest atheists will admit they cannot prove God does not exist.[37]

The question then becomes; how can we know God exists if we have never seen Him? First, we believe the Bible, which declares that He exists. As Christians, at an experiential level, we know God exists because we speak to Him every day. We do not audibly hear Him speaking to us, but we sense His presence, we feel His leading, we know His love, we desire His grace. We can reflect on things that have occurred in our lives that have no possible explanation other than God. When we reflect on what we used to be, how we used to act, and how God has so miraculously saved us and changed our lives that we cannot help but acknowledge and praise His existence.

None of these arguments can persuade anyone who refuses to acknowledge what is already obvious. In the end, God's existence must be accepted by faith. *But without faith it is impossible to please Him, for he who comes to God must believe that He is, and that He is a rewarder of those who diligently seek Him."* Faith in God is not a blind leap into the dark; it is safe step into a well-lit room where the clear majority of people are already standing.[38]

- We know there is a Creator because of creation.
- We know there is a lawgiver because of laws.
- We know there is a moral absolute because of our conscience.
- We know there is a God because of the Bible.
- We know there is salvation because of Jesus the Savior.

REFLECTIONS AND MEDITATIONS

1. As a believer, how does believing there is a God affect your living responsibly in this world?

CHAPTER 5

"THE BEST BET: EXHIBIT B"

"But without faith it is impossible to please Him, for he who comes to God must believe that He is, and that He is a rewarder of those who diligently seek Him." (Hebrews 11:6)

In Exhibit A, despite what has been shared, no matter how many attempts or what proofs we may show, each of us needs to take a moment to stop and think deeply about this matter.

There was once a philosopher by the name of Blaise Pascal who wrote what are call the Pensées. Therein, he wrote what was called "The Wager." The Wager is not an attempt to prove that God exists. It is not a new argument for the existence of God. Rather it tries to prove that it is eminently reasonable for anyone to "bet" on God, to hope that God is, and to invest his life in God. He said, "I should be much more afraid of being mistaken and then finding out that Christianity is true than of being mistaken in believing it to be true." [39]

PASCAL'S WAGER

Pascal's Wager is named after 17th-century French philosopher and mathematician Blaise Pascal. One of Pascal's most famous works was the Pensées ("Thoughts"), which was published posthumously in 1670. It is in this work that we find what is known as Pascal's Wager.[40]

The gist of the Wager is that, according to Pascal, one cannot come to the knowledge of God's existence through reason alone, so the wise thing to do is to live your life as if God does exist because such a life has everything to gain and nothing to lose. If we live as though God exists, and He does indeed exist, we have gained heaven. If He doesn't exist, we have lost nothing. If, on the other hand, we live as though God does not exist and He really does exist, we have gained hell and punishment and have lost heaven and bliss. If one weighs the options, clearly the rational choice to live as if God exists is the better of the possible choices. Pascal even suggested that some may not, at the time, have the ability to believe in God. In such a case, one should live as if he had faith anyway. Perhaps living as if one had faith may lead one to actually come to faith. [41]

"We can be wrong in two ways: by "wagering" on God when there is no God or by "wagering" on there being no God when there is a God. The second mistake loses everything, the first loses nothing. The second is therefore the stupidest wager in the world, and the first the wisest." [42]

"We can also be right in two ways: by wagering on God when there is a God or by wagering on no God when is there is no God. If we are right in the first, we gain everything; if we are right in the second way, we gain nothing, for there is nothing to gain. Therefore, the first is the world's wisest wager and second is the stupidest." [43]

"Either God is or He is not." "Objectively, there are only two possibilities either God exists or not. Subjectively, there are only two possibilities: either I believe, or not. Thus, combining the two sets of variables, we get four possibilities:

1. God exists and I believe in Him
2. God exists and I do not believe in Him.
3. God does not exist and I believe in Him.
4. God does not exist and I do not believe in Him. [44]

"The only choice of winning the happiness we crave—adequate, total, eternal, unending, unlimited, infinite happiness—is the first of the four possibilities delineated above, namely, the combination "God exists and I believe." And the only possibility of losing this happiness and finding eternal unhappiness is possibility number 2, "God exists and I do not believe." In possibilities numbered 3 and number 4, there is no God, and therefore no eternity, no Heaven and no Hell, no reward and no punishment, nothing to win and nothing to lose, no payoff for the wager." [45]

"Reason cannot decide this question." "If theoretical, objective, logical, scientific reason could decide this question, we would not need to wager. If we had proof, we would not need to take a chance. The Wager is addressed only to those who are not convinced that reason can prove theism (God) or atheism (God does not exist.)" [46]

"At death we will find the coin of life coming down in one of two ways either "heads. . . you see God face to face—or "tails" ---God's retreat, God's death, God's nonexistence. At death, you find out which of the two possibilities is true, atheism or theism." [47] "But now, before death, you must choose to believe one way or the other. Both theism and atheism are leaps of faith, bets, wagers, chances." [48]

"We cannot choose whether or not we must choose. We must choose, though we are free to choose unbelief or belief." [49]

"Why can't we choose not to choose? Why can't we choose agnosticism? Because we are "already committed," that is, "embarked," as on a ship. The ship is our life. The sea is time. We are moving, past a port that claims to be our true home. We can choose to turn and put in at this port (that is, to believe) or to refuse it (that is, to disbelieve), but we cannot choose to stay motionless at sea. For we are not motionless, we are dying." [50]

"Our journey, and our fuel, is finite. Someday soon the fuel will run out and we will no longer be able to choose to put in at the port of God, to believe, for we will have no more time. There is a point of no return. In other words, to every possible question life presents three possible answers: Yes, No, and Evasion. Death removes the third answer." [51]

"This "home port," you see, is not just an idea (that God exists). It is a marriage proposal from this God. Not to say Yes is eventually to say No. Suppose Romeo proposes to Juliet, and she says neither Yes nor No, but Wait. Suppose the "wait" last—until she dies. There her "wait" becomes No. Death turns agnosticism into atheism. For death turns "Tomorrow" into "Never." Once this is clear, the choice must be made, that there are only two alternatives, not three, the next step is easy." [52]

"Truth faith is not a wager but a relationship. But it can begin with a wager, just as a marriage can begin with a blind date." [53]

"Remember, it is not an argument for the existence of God but an argument for faith. Its conclusion is not "Therefore God exists" but "Therefore you should believe." [54]

Now there have been criticisms over the years from various camps. For example, there is the argument from inconsistent revelations. This argument critiques Pascal's Wager on the basis that there is no reason to limit the choices to the Christian God. Since there have been many religions throughout human history, there can be many potential gods. Another critique comes from atheist circles. Richard Dawkins postulated the possibility of a god that might reward honest disbelief and punish blind or feigned faith.

CAN PASCAL'S WAGER BE SQUARED WITH SCRIPTURE?

The Wager fails on several counts. First and foremost, it doesn't consider the apostle Paul's argument in Romans 1 that the knowledge of God is evident to all so that we are without excuse (Romans 1:19-20). Reason alone can bring us to the knowledge of God's existence. It will be an incomplete knowledge of God, but it is the knowledge of God nonetheless. Furthermore, the knowledge of God is enough to render us all without excuse before God's judgment. We are all under God's wrath for suppressing the truth of God in unrighteousness (Romans 1:18).

Second, there is no mention of the cost involved in following Jesus. In the gospel of Luke, Jesus twice warns us to count the costs of becoming His disciple (Luke 9:57-62; 14:25-33). There is a cost to following Jesus, and it is not an easy price to pay. Jesus told His disciples that they would have to lose their lives in order to save them (Matthew 10:39). Following Jesus brings with it the hatred of the world (John 15:19). Pascal's Wager makes no mention of any of this. As such, it reduces faith in Christ to trusting without proper or adequate evidence.

Third, it completely misrepresents the depravity of human nature. The natural man—one who has not been born again by the Holy Spirit (John 3:3)—cannot be persuaded to a saving faith in Jesus Christ by a cost-benefit analysis such as Pascal's Wager. Faith is a result of being born again and that is a divine work of the Holy Spirit. This is not to say that one cannot assent to the facts of the gospel or even be outwardly obedient to the law of God. One of the points from Jesus' parable of the soils (Matthew 13) is that false conversions are going to be a fact of life until the time Christ returns. However, the sign of true saving faith is the fruit it produces (Matthew 7:16-20). Paul makes the argument that the natural man cannot understand the things of God (1 Corinthians 2:14). Why? Because they are spiritually discerned. Pascal's Wager makes no mention of the necessary preliminary work of the Spirit to come to the knowledge of saving faith.

Fourth and finally, as an apologetic/evangelistic tool (which is what the Wager was intended to be), it seems focused on a risk/reward outlook, which is not consistent to a true saving faith relationship in Christ. Jesus placed obedience to His commands as an evidence of love for Christ (John 14:23). According to Pascal's Wager, one is choosing to believe and obey God based on receiving heaven as a reward. This is not to diminish the fact that heaven is a reward and that it is something we should hope for and desire. But if our obedience is solely, or primarily, motivated by wanting to get into heaven and avoid hell, then faith and obedience become a means of achieving what we want rather than the result of a heart that has been reborn in Christ and expresses faith and obedience out of love of Christ.

In conclusion, Pascal's Wager, while an interesting piece of philosophical thought, should have no place in a Christian's evangelistic and apologetic repertoire. Christians are to share and proclaim the gospel of Jesus Christ, which alone is the "power of God for salvation to everyone who believes" (Romans 1:16).

DO WE BELIEVE ONLY TO RECEIVE?

> *"But without faith it is impossible to please Him, for he who comes to God must believe that He is, and that He is a rewarder of those who diligently seek Him."* (Hebrews 11:6)

Everywhere we look people offer us rewards if we buy this or shop at their store, or buy petrol at certain petrol stations. We are rewarded on our credit card if we buy a certain amount using their card. People at the Super Market ask, "Do you have a Rewards Card?" Buy one get one free.

In the matter of the spiritual, does this seem wrong. Surely heaven is enough reward and besides, if all sin is regarded as the same and deserving of hell, how can good deeds then be rated on a scale, and rewarded accordingly. In heaven, we will not have a desire to sin anymore! What could be more rewarding than that? And why would other rewards be necessary?[55]

Paul talks about rewards, Peter talks about rewards, John talks about rewards. The reward factor in the Christian experience is a fact of life, and it was recognized and promoted by the Lord Himself. It is abundantly clear that Jesus did not hesitate to speak in terms of rewards and punishment, so let's not become more spiritual on the subject then Jesus was.[56]

There are churches today that preach that anything less than prosperity is failure and God wants nothing to do with failure. Now somewhere along the line the gospel has gotten confused with the American Dream, and there is nothing wrong with the

American Dream, a little hard work and the desire to succeed never hurt anyone, but it's not the Gospel. This is important, spiritual success does not necessarily guarantee success. Now often the touch of God upon a person's life improves their self-image and gives them the gumption to do more for their family, but Christ does not save us to make us rich. He never promised us wealth. You say what does He promise then, well He promised persecution, hardship, a cross, mockery and the grace to see us through those times. [57]

The question is what rewards are you looking for?

****

Many people read Hebrews 11:1, and have no Bible knowledge whatsoever as to what it means, so they look at faith like it's a lucky rabbits foot; it's not luck.

- Faith is something hoped for, it's not a lucky rabbits foot as some call it.
- Faith is not crossing your fingers and walking through life hoping everything will be alright.
- Faith is not playing the odds.
- Faith is not playing the gospel lottery.[58]

Faith is in God, and the hope for the believer is based upon the Word of God. Therefore, faith is believing God will do, and He will do it for you. Therefore:

- I don't hope that God answers prayers, I know He will answer prayers, because He answered yours and mine.
- I don't hope God heals, I know that He will heal, because He healed some of us.
- I don't hope God leads, guides and provides, I know He leads, guides and provides, because He's doing it right now.
- I don't hope there's life after death, I know there's life after death, because my God lives, and because He lives, I have faith.

- I don't hope He's coming again, I know He's coming again, because the Bible says, "that this same Jesus, shall come in like manner, just as you have seen Him go". [59]

So, pickup, pack up, look up, and be prayed up, because we're going up in a twinkling of an eye.

Where there is faith we . . . See the invisible, Believe the Incomprehensible, Hear the inaudible, Feel the intangible, Expect the impossible, Hope the imperishable.

REFLECTIONS AND MEDITATIONS

1. What is your motivation in believing there is a God?
2. Are you betting there is a God or have you truly been born again?

CHAPTER 6

"WHAT SAY YOU?"

"He said to them, "But who do you say that I am?"
(Matthew 16:15)

Unlike the question "Does God exist?" very few people question whether Jesus Christ existed. It is generally accepted that Jesus was truly a man who walked on the earth in Israel more than 2,000 years ago. The debate begins when the subject of Jesus' full identity is discussed. Almost every major religion teaches that Jesus was a prophet or a good teacher or a godly man or a good moral teacher. The problem is that the Bible tells us that Jesus was infinitely more than a prophet, a good teacher, or a godly man, or a good moral teacher; He is God!

In our text, Jesus asked, *"Who do you say that I am?"* Jesus is never recorded in the Bible as saying the precise words, "I am God." That does not mean, however, that He did not proclaim that He is God, as evidenced by statements like that which appears in John 10:30, *"I and the Father are one."* We need only to look at the Jews' reaction to His statement to know He was claiming to be God. *"The Jews took up stones again to stone Him"* (vs. 31).

C. S. Lewis in his book *Mere Christianity* writes the following in response to those who accept Jesus as a great moral teacher, but don't accept his claim to be God. *"A man who was merely a man and said the sort of things Jesus said would not be a great moral teacher.*

He would either be a lunatic—on a level with a man who says he is a poached egg—or else he would be the Devil of hell. You must make your choice. Either this man was, and is, the Son of God, or else a madman or something worse. You can shut Him up for a fool, you can spit at Him and kill Him as a demon; or you can fall at His feet and call Him Lord and God. But let us not come up with any patronizing nonsense about His being a great human teacher. He has not left that option open to us. He did not intend to.[60]

Each of us must decide as to who Jesus is. He is either a liar, a lunatic, or we fall at His feet and call Him Lord and God.

JESUS KNEW WHO HE WAS

When Jesus came into the region of Caesarea Philippi, He asked His disciples, saying, "Who do men say that I, the Son of Man, am?" (vs. 13)

In this verse, Jesus asks His disciples who the people say that He is, while at the same time knowing who He was. *"Who do men say that I, the Son of Man, am?"* Jesus understood very clearly who He was, His question was regarding the perception that the masses had of who He was, and as we shall see, more importantly, who the disciples understood Him to be.

Jesus is referred to as the "Son of Man" 88 times in the New Testament. A first meaning of the phrase "Son of Man" is as a reference to the prophecy of Daniel 7:13-14 (NIV); *"In my vision at night I looked, and there before me was one like a son of man, coming with the clouds of heaven. He approached the Ancient of Days and was led into His presence. He was given authority, glory and sovereign power; all peoples, nations and men of every language worshiped Him. His dominion is an everlasting dominion that will not pass away, and His kingdom is one that will never be destroyed."* The description "Son of Man" was a Messianic title. When Jesus used this phrase, He was assigning Daniel's Son of Man prophecy to Himself and thus He was the recipient and possessor of all *authority, glory and sovereign power.* The Jews of that era would have been intimately familiar with the phrase and to whom it referred. Jesus was proclaiming Himself as the Messiah.[61]

A second meaning of the phrase "Son of Man" is that Jesus was truly a human being. God called the prophet Ezekiel "son of man" 93 times. God was simply calling Ezekiel a human being. A son of a man is a man. Jesus was fully God (John 1:1), but He was also a human being (John 1:14). First John 4:2 tells us, *"This is how you can recognize the Spirit of God: Every spirit that acknowledges that Jesus Christ has come in the flesh is from God."* Yes, Jesus was the Son of God—He was in His Essence God. Yes, Jesus was also the Son of Man—He was in His essence a human being. In summary, the phrase "Son of Man" indicates that Jesus is the Messiah and that He is truly a human being.[62]

THE PEOPLE IDENTIFIED HIM BY COMPARISON

> *"So they said, "Some say John the Baptist, some Elijah, and others Jeremiah or one of the prophets."*
> (vs. 14)

One day a teacher asked her fourth grade class this question: "Who is the greatest human being alive in the world today?" The responses came quickly. One boy said, "I think it's Tiger Woods. He's the best golfer ever." A girl said, "I think it's the Pope because he cares for people and doesn't get paid for it all." A very wise and perceptive student responded, "It's Brett Favre because he's coming back for the Pack." The kids shouted out one celebrity after another until Donnie spoke up: "I think it's Jesus Christ because He loves everybody and is always ready to help them." The teacher told him that his answer was OK but that she was looking for the greatest living person, and of course Jesus lived and died almost two thousand years ago. To which Donnie replied, "Oh no, Mrs. Thompson, that's not true at all. Jesus Christ is alive and He lives in me right now! "He got the answer right, didn't he? [63] Jesus is the greatest person who lived and is living.

In response to Jesus question, the disciples declared that the people sought to define who Jesus was by historical personalities. In their minds, He must be someone of importance, but not only of importance, but of spiritual importance. We don't know who these were who answered this question but four answers bubbled to the surface:

- John the Baptist. Since John had been held in high honor by the people, some thought that he had come back to life.
- Elijah. Hundreds of years earlier, the prophet Elijah exposed what was in human hearts, performed miracles and inspired people; since Jesus could do these same things, maybe He was really Elijah.
- Jeremiah. This prophet was known to speak boldly and yet mourn over the hardness of people's hearts. People saw Jesus pronounce woes and weep and so they wondered if He was Jeremiah.
- One of the prophets. Others could not decide and so they thought He must be another prophet who had come back to life.

Their answer in many ways affirmed their belief of life after death and of resurrection. For if He was indeed any of those whom they perceived Him to be, Old Testament personalities and prophets, He would have had to come back from the grave.

The disciples knew what people were saying about Jesus and they could summarize these beliefs. However, they all fell short of the real answer. These were not bad answers in themselves but they all fell short of who Jesus is because no one was openly confessing that Jesus Christ was the Messiah.

Although Jesus did similar deeds to those in the past, He was greater than them all. When He referred to Himself as *the Son of man*, He set Himself apart; He sanctified Himself, as more than any of those mentioned. *The Son of man* was the way that Jesus described Himself that was indicative of both humanity and divinity.

In our day people compare Jesus to Buddha, Mohammed, Gandhi, Confucius, and other spiritual personalities. But none of them were God, none came from heaven, all are dead and gone, never to return. Jesus on the other hand lives and sits at the right hand of God awaiting His return. The resurrection sets Jesus apart from all His earthly comparisons. The resurrection was and is the crowning element that makes Him like none other.

SIMON PETER SUPERNATURALLY DECLARED WHO HE WAS

> *"Simon Peter answered and said, "You are the Christ, the Son of the living God." Jesus answered and said to him, "Blessed are you, Simon Bar-Jonah, for flesh and blood has not revealed this to you, but My Father who is in heaven. "And I also say to you that you are Peter, and on this rock I will build My church, and the gates of Hades shall not prevail against it."* (vs. 16-18)

Simon Peter declared the truth about who Jesus was. He *"said, "You are the Christ, the Son of the living God."* In Jesus response to Peter's declaration, He says that Peter *spoke better than he knew, for flesh and blood has not revealed this to you.* The disclosure of who Jesus was, was by God's revelation. Although Peter had seen Jesus work miracles, the fullness and realization of who He was had not come to bear. The death, burial, and resurrection were events yet to come.

Peter declared that Jesus was *the Christ, the Son of the living God.* The name *Christ*, the anointed one, is the official title of Jesus, occurring over 520 times in the New Testament. It means that He was anointed as the Messiah and Savior. There were three types of people who were anointed in the Old Testament: prophets, priests, and kings. And in Jesus, we find all three.[64]

It is interesting that Jesus changes the disciple's name from Simon Bar-Jonah, meaning Simon son of Jonah, to Peter. Peter was living up to his name (it means "rock") that Jesus had prophetically declared when he first met him. When the Lord and Peter first met, Jesus had said Simon would be named Cephas (Aramaic for "rock") or Peter (Greek for "rock").[65] John 1:42 declares, *"You are Simon the son of Jonah. You shall be called Cephas (which is translated, A Stone)."* Beginning in Acts 2:14, we see the fulfillment of Jesus prophecy, in that we see Peter stand up and declare the gospel that would be the foundational sermon whereby the church would be birthed.

In giving him a new name, Jesus was praising Peter for his accurate statement about Him, and was introducing His work of building the church on Himself (1 Cor. 3:11) and declaring the sufficiency of the gospel, *and the gates of Hades shall not prevail against it.* Jews would understand Hades' gates to refer to physical death. Jesus was thus telling the disciples that even death would not prevent His work of building the church. The fullness of what was yet to be seen and understood by them.

WE MUST KNOW WHO AND WHOSE WE ARE

Many people name their children with little regard to what impact it may have on their lives. If we believe, as they did in biblical times, that all names have meaning, we have to wonder if children are being given names that are harmful. For instance, we would never name one of our children Nabal (which means fool-even though it might become fitting for them as an adult), or Jezebel (the evil and wicked adulteress of the Old Testament), or Jemima (reflective of the days of slavery and Jim Crow). We would not name our child Iddi (reflective of the dictator Iddi Amin), or Ben Lauden (and we surely understand why), or Hussein (as Barak Obama might testify, though innocent enough, has come to have its problems). There are just certain names not befitting of anyone that are problematic. We need to be cautious, do some research, because what we name our child may be reflective of a group of persons, who have committed capital crimes, are prone to mental illness, murder, or a host of other maladies. We may label them with something that sounds, pretty, unique, jazzy, or whatever, but if they live up to their name; we, as parents, would be deeply saddened. A name is significant, meaningful, often reflects the character of a person, and therefore needs to be chosen carefully.

Jesus asked, "*Who do you say that I am?*" This was not about His name, Jesus, it was more about who He was. We must also know who we are. Although we may be called by different names, we "are" Christians. Christians ought not to be something that we are just called. It is indicative of who we are. It is our spiritual identity. Others may choose to label us otherwise, but if we have committed our lives to Jesus as Lord and Savior, we are no longer who we used to be, we are reborn, like Peter we have been given a new name, we are a new creation in Christ Jesus. We cannot and will not let life's circumstances redefine who we are. We are Christians. We are no longer sinners, but saints. We are the children of God. We belong to God.

Many times, as Christians, we are pressured to deny who we are. Many times, as Christians, we compromise our position because to affirm who we are may cause us to meet the wrath of our enemies. We fear that to affirm who we are may cause us to be put down. May cause us to be forsaken by our friends and associates, and possibly, cause us the loss of a promising future.

We live in a day where our affirmation of who we are is being challenged. We are being challenged to deny who and whose we are by those who would exclude the name of God out of the pledge of allegiance, from out of our prayers, off the face of our money, and in the placement of historical symbols (such as the 10 commandments) of our faith. We are being challenged to deny our traditional and biblical understanding of marriage and family. We are being challenged to deny who we are in every area of our lives. If we affirm who and whose we are, if we stand up for truth in all situations, if we affirm who and whose we are in all our endeavours, we may reap the wrath of those around us, because who we and what we are makes them uncomfortable.

Nevertheless, despite what it appears it may cost us we must lift the standard high. We must affirm who and whose we are.

Whatever it costs us; we must not be ashamed to own Him or His words; and even in difficult times confess Christ crucified.

Jesus question was one related to His identity. There are several methods by which we are identified.

- We all have a name; this bag of flesh, bones, and blood was labelled by our parents at the time of our birth. You may not like or agree with what you are called, but that is what you have been labelled.
- We can be identified by others according to our deeds: hero, liar, thief, and whoremonger; or according to our position: pastor, priest, judge, officer, etc.
- People often label us according to our physical ability, or lack thereof: speedy, lazy, unconcerned, bitter.
- People unfortunately are often identified by their nationality: black, white, Asian, Hispanic.

Names are very important, and what we call each other is important. Parents must be careful to not at an early age define what their children are according to how they act, for they might be determined to live up to it. However, we must not be defined by the way we act, the color of our skin, or our abilities or lack thereof. Our real identity is in Christ.

****

Why is the question over Jesus' identity so important? Why does it matter whether Jesus is God? The most important reason that Jesus has to be God is that if He is not God, His death would not have been sufficient to pay the penalty for the sins of the whole world (1 John 2:2). Only God could pay such an infinite penalty (Romans 5:8; 2 Corinthians 5:21). Jesus had to be God so that He could pay our debt. Jesus had to be man so He could die. Salvation is available only through faith in Jesus Christ. Jesus' deity is why He is the only way of salvation. Jesus' deity is why He proclaimed,

"I am the way and the truth and the life. No one comes to the Father except through me" (John 14:6).

It's important to know what others say about Jesus; but it is imperative to know what you personally believe! You won't be held accountable for what others think of Jesus, but you will be eternally accountable for what you think and what you do about it. How you answer the question of who Jesus is will affect both your life, and your afterlife. It must become deeply personal because we all need a personal relationship with Christ.

There is an exam coming for all of us. The good thing is that we have the question ahead of time: *Who do you say that I am?* To be almost right about Jesus is to be totally wrong. Romans 10:9-10 give us the answer, *"That if you confess with your mouth, 'Jesus is Lord,' and believe in your heart that God raised him from the dead, you will be saved. For it is with your heart that you believe and are justified, and it is with your mouth that you confess and are saved."* Are you ready to commit to Christ and then confess that He is your Savior and Lord?[66]

Will you affirm that you are a child of God? Will you affirm what you believe in the face of a world that is challenging you not to believe? Or, will you for fear deny the Christ and who and whose you are?

REFLECTIONS AND MEDITATIONS

1. Who we believe Jesus is affects our potential and power to have victory over the forces of evil.
2. Will you stand up for who you are?

CHAPTER 7

"TRANSFORMED LIVES"

"Peter said to Him, "Even if I have to die with You,
I will not deny You!" And so said all the disciples."
(Matthew 26:35)

In the previous chapter, "What Say You"; we read of the people and Peter's responses to Jesus' question, *"Who do men say that I, the Son of Man, am?"* (Matthew 16:13). The people had compared Him to *John the Baptist, Elijah, Jeremiah, or one of the prophets."* Peter correctly declared, by divine inspiration, Jesus to be *"the Christ, the Son of the living God."*

In later chapters, as Jesus dismisses His disciples from the "last supper," He speaks of His crucifixion, their falling away, and denial of association with him. Peter speaks boldly, as he was oft given to do, saying, *"to Him, "Even if I have to die with You, I will not deny You!"*

We often miss the fact that not only Peter, but as the Scripture declares, *"so said all the disciples."* The warning of Peter's three-time denial by Jesus is well acknowledged in biblical history. Seemingly, Peter was the only one brave enough to follow Jesus to the place of inquisition, the courtyard of the high priest Caiaphas, but we can be sure that as Jesus declared the others were just as fearful as he, and in some way also denied relationship with Him. Those who had walked, talked, ate, slept, and lived with Jesus for three years all fell away.

When we observe the disciple's commitment to Jesus before His crucifixion and afterwards, we see a remarkable transformation. They go from being timid, fearful, and denying relationship with Him to boldly proclaiming their relationship to the point of being willing to suffer and even die for the cause of Christ.

If there is any evidence to which we can lean apart from the declaration of the Word itself to answer the question is Jesus God, it is this transformation of the disciples from being mere followers to being men who were willing to be martyrs, to give their very lives.

When we think about the person of Jesus and whether He was God, it seems that one of the greatest proofs is His disciples were willing to be martyred for their beliefs in Him and that the gospel has continued to propagate throughout time.

THE INITIAL FOUNDATION OF THE DISCIPLES BELIEF WAS THE MIRACLES

> *"Men of Israel, hear these words: Jesus of Nazareth, a Man attested by God to you by miracles, wonders, and signs which God did through Him in your midst, as you yourselves also know--" Him, being delivered by the determined purpose and foreknowledge of God, you have taken by lawless hands, have crucified, and put to death; "whom God raised up, having loosed the pains of death, because it was not possible that He should be held by it."* (Acts 2:22-24)

These words are the opening words of Peter's sermon on the Day of Pentecost, a day that would see 3,000 souls saved. It was his reflective testimony of who they observed Jesus to be. Peter declares that Jesus was *"a Man attested by God to you by miracles, wonders, and signs which God did through Him in your midst, as you yourselves also know."* Jesus set Himself apart from the prophets and holy men of His day through the performance of signs and wonders. It was His

- turning water to wine (John 2:7).
- walking on water (Matthew 14:25).
- multiplying physical objects (John 6:11).
- healing the blind (John 9:7).
- healing the lame (Mark 2:3).
- healing the sick (Matthew 9:35; Mark 1:40-42).
- and even raising people from the dead (John 11:43-44; Luke 7:11-15; Mark 5:35).

that established He was someone different.

The disciple's faith, as Peter here declares, was initially the product of what they had seen and heard.

Neither the disciples, nor the people, were sure, but they acknowledged that His connection to God was something different than they had ever seen. Their faith was in the physical manifestations' that Jesus had performed. That is why they scattered and were not committed to stand with Him during times of His arrest, trial, and crucifixion. Even those who acknowledged Him as God, were not sure what that meant to their personal future and the future of the nation.

THE TRANSFORMATION FROM
FOLLOWERS TO MARTYRS

How do we explain what happened to the 12 disciples? Jesus' first and closest followers. They were with Him throughout His ministry but when Jesus was arrested and the whole thing seemed to be coming apart they scattered. Peter three times strongly denied his connection to Jesus. They didn't want to be persecuted. They didn't want to suffer. They separated themselves from Jesus because they didn't want to go down with the ship.

There was a remarkable transformation that occurred in those who were followers of Jesus. Before the cross, they are timid, fearful, and unsure. Peter denied Him, the other disciples deserted Him. What was the source of their transformation?

The greatest miracle, the greatest proof of the deity of God, is that Christ Himself rose from the dead. Christ proved His claims to deity through miracles, the greatest of which was the world-altering resurrection. No other theory can explain why there was a significant transformation of the disciples. Following the resurrection, we find a renewed sense of courage where they are willing to be flogged, stoned, and slain, for the cause of Christ.

There have always been people who are willing to die for what they believe; that fact is nothing new. Soldiers on the battlefield daily give their lives for the cause of our freedom. Many of those who followed Jim Jones were willing to die in what Jones said was an act of "revolutionary suicide" at the Jamestown Massacre (1978) because they believed in him and his message. There are Muslims who become suicide bombers, more properly considered martyrs, believing that as they kill infidels, that they are doing the will of Allah.

The question for each of us is would we be willing to die for the cause of Christ and Christianity? That is the real test of who we believe Jesus is, what we believe about the Bible, and about God. Do we follow Him for the sake of miracles, for what we have gotten or expect to get from Him, or does it go somewhere deeper? Is it about miracles, signs, and wonders?

THE TESTIMONY OF MARTYRDOM

The only apostle whose death the Bible records is James (Acts 12:2). King Herod had James *"put to death with the sword,"* likely a reference to beheading. The circumstances of the deaths of the other apostles are related through church tradition. The early church fathers, such as Hippolytus and Eusebius, record that the deaths of the disciples were such that they were without a doubt convinced that Jesus was God.

- The most commonly accepted church tradition regarding the death of an apostle is that the apostle Peter was crucified upside-down on an x-shaped cross in Rome in fulfillment of Jesus' prophecy (John 21:18).

The following are the most popular "traditions" concerning the deaths of the other apostles: [67]

- Matthew suffered martyrdom in Ethiopia, killed by a sword wound.
- John faced martyrdom when he was boiled in a huge basin of boiling oil during a wave of persecution in Rome. However, he was miraculously delivered from death. He died as an old man, the only apostle to die peacefully.
- James, the brother of Jesus (not officially an apostle), was thrown from the southeast pinnacle of the temple (over a hundred feet down) when he refused to deny his faith in Christ.
- Bartholomew, also known as Nathanael, was flayed to death by a whip.
- Andrew was crucified on an x-shaped cross in Greece.
- The apostle Thomas was stabbed with a spear in India during one of his missionary trips to establish the church there.
- Matthias, the apostle chosen to replace the traitor Judas Iscariot, was stoned and then beheaded.
- The apostle Paul was tortured and then beheaded by the evil Emperor Nero in Rome in A.D. 67.

Something incredible happened to the disciples. They went from frightened cowards to witnesses for Christ so bold that the threat of death held no affect. If they wanted to be comfortable and safe and free from persecution all they had to do was shut up. If they would have stopped preaching about Jesus no one would have bothered them. But they couldn't do that. Something happened.

It is not so important how the apostles died. What is important is the fact that they were all willing to die for their faith. The transformation of the disciples is one clear evidence that if they had any doubts as to who He was, the resurrection clearly destroyed them all.

If Jesus had not been resurrected, the disciples would have known it. People will not die for something they know to be a lie. The fact that all the apostles were willing to die horrible deaths, refusing to renounce their faith in Christ, is tremendous evidence that they had truly witnessed the resurrection of Jesus Christ.

BELIEVERS ARE STILL DYING FOR THEIR FAITH!

We claim Jesus as Lord, Savior, and God, but are we convinced to the point of being willing to die for our beliefs? Some are thinking, I'm so glad stuff like that doesn't happen today. But the reality is, that is still happening today. In many countries, persecution is common place. Here are some facts for you:

Brother Andrew, founder of the mission agency Open Doors, in his 1967 book *God's Smuggler*, which has sold tens of millions of copies around the globe[68], wrote, "The past century is known as "The martyrs' century" because more people have lost their lives for their Christianity since 1900 than in all the previous centuries together."

Michael Horowitz of the Hudson Institute writes, "All over the world there are about 200 million followers of Christ suffering today," "and it's surprising that nobody, neither the Christian community nor the establishment, talks about it." [69] He writes, "At Sudan's market you can buy a young Christian slave starting with only two chickens."

Torture and arrest are becoming part of daily life in the Muslim world. In Saudi Arabia, there is a special religious police whose job it is to search private houses and make arrests, confiscating Bibles as well as tapes with religious recordings. [70]

Nina Shea a former director of the Center for Religious Freedom at Freedom House, the oldest human rights group in the

U.S. and director of the Hudson Institute's Center for Religious Freedom informs us that the Muslim world is not the only place where Christians are persecuted. "In China many thousands of those who profess Christ live in religious gulags." She explains, "they are imprisoned and tortured simply because they dared to pray; sing hymns and read the Bible in public places". Chinese prisons hold more Christians than any other country of the world.[71]

Christians are also persecuted in North Korea, Saudi Arabia, Somalia, Yemen, Laos, Nigeria, Cuba, and more and more now in Iraq, Afghanistan, Pakistan, India, and many other places. Most estimates range from 150,000 killed each year and up—more than 15 every hour. [72]

Here in America, religious persecution is widespread, but subtle . . . in mostly non-violent forms, for now! The American Christians' idea of persecution is:

• Losing a job because you won't compromise your convictions.
• being passed over for promotion.
• people sneering and jeering for your witness.
• having a door slammed in their face on visitation.
• a friend laughs at them if they witness to them.

Churches in America have had it relatively easy for two reasons:

1. It's still a semi-free country.
2. We're not witnessing or taking a stand for Christ! [73]

However, as we approach the end of the world, though we will not go thru the tribulation, Jesus made it clear that the shadow of things to come will fall upon us in the form of perilous times. And America may very well face extreme persecution of Christians in the future. After all, we're already spoken of in terms of divisive hate...terms like "homophobic, out of touch with society, radical right wing, conservative fundamentalists, born again extremists"! [74]

Be not deceived the world is not our friend. Jesus said in John 17:14, *"I have given them Your word; and the world has hated them because they are not of the world, just as I am not of the world."*

****

The story is told that many years ago, when communism still held the Soviet Union in its iron clench, a little group of Christians met behind closed doors in the underground. This was a secret meeting, a secret church service.

Suddenly, the doors burst open, and two soldiers appeared with sub-machine guns. They shouted, "To all those who are willing to renounce Jesus Christ: You've got five minutes to leave! Everyone who remains will be shot immediately."

As you can imagine, every Christian in that place began to search their heart, and ask themselves, Am I willing to die for Jesus Christ right now, today?

A few got up and left, ashamedly, quietly, they left with heads hung low. Most of the people stayed. As the last one left, a soldier shouted, is that it? He held up his gun and repeated, anyone else? Another man rose and ran out. The soldiers locked the doors, and turned toward the people . . . they laid down their guns . . . and said, "Brothers and Sisters, we too are Christians. We do not want to worship the Lord with anyone who is not willing to die for Him! Now that the half-hearted have gone, let's have church!" What a service they had together that day![75]

We need to ask ourselves today, what if those soldiers burst into the doors of your church, your gathering right now; would I stay, or would I leave?

What if you were put on the rack, and asked to renounce your faith?

- roasted on the gridiron.
- scalded with water.
- whipped or beaten.
- flayed alive.

- your family threatened?

I don't believe any of us can know what we would do in that moment, though we hope we would not shame our Savior. However, there is one strong indication you can look for, which will very much measure how likely you are to be willing to die for Christ, and that is, are you living for Him now?

- If your faith won't bring you back to God's house regularly, it is highly unlikely it would take you to the gas chamber, if called upon.
- A faith that does not bring words of witness to your lips in our land of free speech would not likely go to a burning stake to be a public testimony for Christ.
- If your faith can't get the 10% our Lord requires out of your pocket, it would not likely get you to the chopping block for beheading!
- If your faith can't keep you away from worldly amusements or can't keep you from fleshly habits, it's not likely it would take you to the lions' den.
- A faith that doesn't prompt you to obey in the smallest of matters like Bible reading and prayer would unlikely bring you before a firing squad. [76]

How do you know if you would die for Christ? For starters, ask are you living for Him? Romans 12:1 declares, *I beseech you therefore, brethren, by the mercies of God, that you present your bodies a living sacrifice, holy, acceptable unto God, which is your reasonable service.* You can know for certain that you will not present yourself as a dying sacrifice if you aren't a living sacrifice right now!

God forgive us today for having half-hearted devotion . . . considering those who've gone before us! Lord, help us to live for you, and if necessary, to die for you!

REFLECTIONS AND MEDITATIONS

1. Who we believe Jesus is affects our potential and power to have victory over the fear of declaring our faith.
2. Are you a living testimony of faith?
3. In what ways has faith in Jesus transformed your life?

CHAPTER 8

"THE HOLY SPIRIT"

"Nevertheless I tell you the truth. It is to your advantage that I go away; for if I do not go away, the Helper will not come to you; but if I depart, I will send Him to you." (John 16:7)

A. W. Tozer once commented that if God were to take the Holy Spirit out of this world, most of what the church is doing would go right on, and nobody would know the difference. [77]

That is a stinging indictment against the church. Part of the problem in our society is that the church has become a religious institution whose machinery runs smoothly without any need of the Holy Spirit. Unfortunately, the same indictment could be made concerning some of our lives. If God were to take the Holy Spirit out of this world what if anything, would change in our lives? How would we find ourselves limited? What are we doing now that could not be done? Would we know, be able to detect the difference?

In the passage before us, Christ gives His disciples assurance of the Holy Spirit's aid in their future work, in the execution of the ministry which they would soon launch. He shared with them that He would go to His Father, but they would not be left alone. Rather, they would have one, a helper, who would continue His ministry in them. Their spiritual education would not stop, school would remain in session, they would continue in a ministry that evidenced the power of God by signs and wonders. In fact, they would move beyond their present level of understanding and spiritual capabilities to new and higher heights. The promise of the Holy Spirit was not given to them without purpose but that they might go forth in the ministry of the Word with power. They would undergo a remarkable transformation. They would go from being timid, fearful, and denying relationship with Him to boldly proclaiming their relationship to the point of being willing to suffer and even die for the cause of Christ.

The Holy Spirit has been given to every believer that the power of God might be activated in our lives, that we may be transformed. To activate this power, we first need to know who this Holy Spirit is and how He is related to us as Christians.

WHO IS THE HOLY SPIRIT?

> *"Nevertheless I tell you the truth. It is to your advantage that I go away; for if I do not go away, the Helper will not come to you; but if I depart, I will send Him to you"* (John 16:7). That was the promise! Fifty days following the Passover the promise would be fulfilled at Pentecost.

When Jesus refers to the Holy Spirit as the Helper, He uses a Greek word, *Paraclete*, that was an ancient warrior's term. Greek soldiers went into battle in pairs, so when the enemy attacked, they could draw together back-to-back, covering each other's blind side. One's battle partner was the *paraclete*. Our Lord does not send us to fight the good fight alone. The Holy Spirit is our battle partner who covers our blind side and fights for our well-being.

The Holy Spirit is the third person of the Trinity: Father, Son and Holy Spirit. The Bible teaches that the Holy Spirit is not a force or thing but a person. The Bible also ascribes to Him the acts we would expect of someone who was not just a force, but a real person.

- He speaks: *"He who has an ear, let him hear what the Spirit says to the churches".* (Rev 2:7)
- He intercedes, for us to God in prayer. (Romans 8:26)
- He testifies, of Christ to us. (John 15:26)
- He leads, us into fruitful endeavors. (Acts 8:29, Romans 8:14)
- He commands, the spiritual decisions of our lives. Acts 16:6, 7)
- He appoints, us as overseers in the work of the Lord. (Acts 20:28)
- He can be lied to, with fatal results, as Ananias and Sapphira came to find out. (Acts 5:3, 4)
- He can be insulted. (Hebrews 10:29)
- He can be blasphemed against, for which there is no forgiveness. (Matt 12:31, 32)
- He can be grieved, by insincerity and inconsistency of those who claim to love the Lord. (Ephesians 4:30)

Each of these emotions and acts are characteristic of a person. The Holy Spirit is not an impersonal force, like gravity or magnetism. He is a person with all the attributes of personality.

However, not only is He a person; He is divine as well. He is God. He is equal in every way with the Father and with the Son. All the divine attributes are ascribed to the Holy Spirit. He has infinite intellect (1 Corinthians 2:11), will (1 Corinthians 12:11), and emotion (Romans 15:30).

The Holy Spirit is one with the Father and one with the Son in the godhead. It is not one, plus one, plus one equals three. It is one, times-one, times-one equals one. Like an egg, that has three parts: shell, white, and a yolk but is still an egg. Like water, which can be ice, liquid, or steam, yet still be water. Like myself; I can be husband to my wife, father to my children, and a son to my parents yet still be me. The Holy Spirit is one with the Father and the Son. First John 5:7 declares, *"For there are three that bear witness in heaven: The Father, the Word, and the Holy Spirit; and these three are one."* If the Father is God, and Jesus is God, then the Holy Spirit is also God; three in one, yet all distinctly different.

WHY DID THE HOLY SPIRIT COME?

> *"And when He has come, He will convict the world of sin, and of righteousness, and of judgment": of sin, because they do not believe in Me; "of righteousness, because I go to My Father and you see Me no more"; of judgment, because the ruler of this world is judged."* (vs. 8-11)

The Spirit's work is twofold. First, He has come to convict the world of sin, righteousness, and judgment (John 16:8-11). The Bible teaches us, and we know from experience, that all have sinned and have come short of the glory of God (Romans 3:23). Sinful people cannot inherit eternal life.

However, an unbeliever may not be consciously aware that their deepest problem is sin. Or, that sin has separated them from fellowship with God. Therefore, it is the work of the Holy Spirit to disturb and convict them in their sin because we will all stand in judgment before God. Until this takes place, they cannot experience salvation. However, the Holy Spirit not only convicts of sin, He convinces us that Jesus is the righteousness of God. He shows sinners that *Jesus is the way, the truth, and the life,* and that no one comes to the Father but by Him. When we witness, we can be assured that it is not totally our effort that will bring a person to Christ.

The Holy Spirit's work in the world is not confined to the ministry of conviction concerning sin, righteousness, and judgment, however. His second work in the world is to hinder the growth of lawlessness, that is, to engage in the ministry of preservation. Verse 13 tells us, *"When He, the Spirit of truth, has come, He will guide you into all truth; for He will not speak on His own authority, but whatever He hears He will speak; and He will tell you things to come."*

This planet would already be a literal hell on earth was it not for the presence of the Holy Spirit in the world. The unbelieving world little knows what it owes to the restraining power of the Holy Spirit. The hand of God is being restrained, for He *desires all men to be saved and to come to the knowledge of the truth.*

The Holy Spirit acts through the people of God, who are called the salt of the earth and the light of the world by Jesus in His Sermon on the Mount. Salt and light speak of the influence Christians can exercise for good in society. They are forces that operate silently and unobstructively, yet with great effect. Salt and light are essential in our homes: light dissipates the darkness, and salt prevents decay. The Bible tells us that the state of the world will grow darker as we near the end of the age. The world has no light of its ownand it is marked by a process of accelerating decay. However, Jesus taught us that we who are His followers act as salt so that we can hinder the process of decline. Christians at work in the world are the only real spiritual light in the midst of a great spiritual darkness.

This places a tremendous responsibility on believers. Only as the world sees our good works do they know that a light is shining. Only as the world senses our moral presence are they conscious of the salt. Therefore, Christ warned against the salt losing its savor, its saltiness, and the light dimming. He said, *"Let you light so shine before men, that they may see your good works, and glorify your Father which is in heaven"* (Matt 5:16). We Christians are not powerless. We have the mighty power of God available through God, the Holy Spirit, even in this world.

HOW IS THE HOLY SPIRIT RELATED TO EVERY CHRISTIAN?

> *"And I will pray the Father, and He will give you another Helper, that He may abide with you forever--"* the Spirit of truth, whom the world cannot receive, because it neither sees Him nor knows Him;

but you know Him, for He dwells with you and will
be in you." (John 14:16, 17)

A Christian is one who has received Jesus Christ into his life as Lord and Savior. At the time of our spiritual birth, the Holy Spirit comes to dwell in us. We become filled with the Holy Spirit. To be filled with the Holy Spirit is to be filled with the one who is already there, in our hearts.

Let me illustrate. If you were to take a sponge and while it is in your hand, squeeze it. In that condition, plunge it in water and submerge it, and keep it in there. It is now in the water but the water is not in it. As you hold it in the water, you open your hand, and as you do so, the water fills all the pores. It is now both in the water and filled with the water. When we receive Christ, we are born anew and like the sponge put into that sphere where the Holy Spirit is operating. As with a sponge when released that soaks up the water, when we open our hearts and allow the light and love of Jesus to come in the Holy Spirit comes to reside in us, to fill us with His presence.

At the time of our spiritual birth, when the Holy Spirit comes in, the Bible tells us:

- The Holy Spirit regenerates us, we become "born again". (John 3:5)
- The Holy Spirit comes to dwell within each of us. (1 Corinthians 3:16; 1 Corinthians 6:19, 20; Romans 8:11)
- The Holy Spirit seals each of us in Christ. (Ephesians 1:13; 4:30)
- The Holy Spirit is the guarantee of salvation that each of us will one day receive. (2 Corinthians 5:5)
- The Holy Spirit baptizes each of us into the Body of Christ. (1 Corinthians 12:13; Galatians 3:27; Romans 6:3, 4; Acts 1:5)
- The Holy Spirit fills every yielded, one of us for service. (Ephesians 5:18-20)

Because of this relationship with Christ, every one of us has the potential to witness with power and to live a life of victory over sin. This potential power, the life of Jesus Christ in every believer, is released by faith as we surrender the control of our life to the Holy Spirit.

A man who drank heavily was converted to Christ and lived victoriously for several weeks. One day as he passed the open door of a tavern, the pungent odor drifting out aroused his old appetite for liquor. Just then he saw this sign in the window of a nearby cafe: "All the buttermilk you can drink -- 25 cents!" Dashing inside, he ordered one glass, then another, and still another. After finishing the third he walked past the saloon and was no longer tempted. He was so full of buttermilk that he had no room for that which would be injurious to him. The lesson is clear; to be victorious over our evil desires, we must leave no opportunity for them to repossess us.

Dwight L. Moody once demonstrated the principle like this: "Tell me," he said to his audience, "How can I get the air out of the glass I have in my hand?" One man said, "Suck it out with a pump." But the evangelist replied, "That would create a vacuum and shatter it." Finally, after many suggestions, Moody picked up a pitcher and quietly filled the glass with water. "There," he said, "all the air is now removed." He then explained that victory for the child of God does not come by working hard to eliminate sinful habits, but rather by allowing the Holy Spirit to take full possession. [78]

The Spirit-filled life is the Christ-filled life. The Spirit-filled Christian is one who, according to Romans 6:11, has considered himself to *be* dead to sin, but alive to God in Jesus Christ. *"Likewise you also, reckon yourselves to be dead indeed to sin, but alive to God in Christ Jesus our Lord"* (Romans 6:11). When we are dead to self, the Lord Jesus Christ, who now has unhindered control of our lives, and can begin to express His love through us.

To be "filled with the Spirit" does not mean that we receive more of the Holy Spirit, but that we give Him more of ourselves. As we yield our lives to the Holy Spirit and are filled with His presence, He has greater freedom to work in and through our lives, to control us to better exalt and glorify Christ.

****

Bill McCartney, founder of Promise Keepers, tells the following story. "When I took the job as head football coach at the University of Colorado in 1982, I made a solemn promise: I told everybody that with me, God was first, family second, and football third.

But I did not keep that promise for long. The thrill and the challenge of resurrecting a football program in disarray simply took too much time and attention. As my teams kept winning year after year, I kept losing focus of my priorities.

When we won the national championship in 1990, many people said I had reached the pinnacle of my profession. But for me, there was emptiness about it. I had everything a man could want, and yet something was missing. I was so busy pursuing my career goals that I was missing out on the Spirit-filled life that God wanted me to have all because I had broken my promise to put God first and foremost in my life." [79]

At the start of this chapter, I asked you. If God were to take the Holy Spirit out of this world what if anything, would change in your life? How would you find yourself limited? What are you doing now that could not be done? Would you know, be able to detect the difference? Bill McCartney is evidence that there can be great success in life apart from God. However, as he testifies, you can miss out on the Spirit-filled life that God wants you to have

With the fulfilment of the promise of the Holy Spirit, the disciples underwent a remarkable transformation. They went from being timid, fearful, and denying relationship with Him to boldly proclaiming their relationship to the point of being willing to suffer and even die for the cause of Christ. We can undergo a transformation as well:

First John 5:14, 15 says, *"Now this is the confidence that we have in Him, that if we ask anything according to His will, He hears us. And if we know that He hears us, whatever we ask, we know that we have the petitions that we have asked of Him."* We know that it is God's will that we be filled with His Spirit. Therefore, as we ask the Holy Spirit to fill us, we can know according to the Word of God that our prayer is answered.

Maybe the Holy Spirit has only been a guest in your life, for He came to live in you the moment you became a Christian. Sometimes He was locked in a small closet, while you used the rest of the house for your pleasure. But I pray that now you want Him to be more than just a guest. In fact, you want to turn the title deed of your life to Him and give Him the keys to every room.

- Invite the Holy Spirit into the library of your mind; He can help you control your negative and nasty thoughts.
- Invite the Holy Spirit into the dining room of your appetites; He can help to control your lustful desires and keep you from compromise.
- Invite the Holy Spirit into the living room of your relationships; He can dispel the darkness of loneliness, feelings of anger, and help you to experience true love.
- Invite the Holy Spirit into the game room of your social life; He will help you find fulfilment and pleasure in things that are wholesome.
- Invite Him to the small hidden rooms where you have previously engaged in secret shameful activities, and He will help you to clean house, dispel the darkness and fill you with the light of His love.

Surrender your life to Him and allow Him to work in you, to fill you with power, to fill you with love, to equip you to share the gospel of Jesus Christ.

This is the good news; we are no longer waiting for the Holy Spirit. He is waiting for us. We are no longer living in a time of promise, but in the days of fulfilment. The Holy Spirit was promised, the promise was fulfilled, the disciples were transformed, and the glory of it for us is that He is present in every true believer today. Therefore, His power is available today to everyone who is yielded unto Him.

REFLECTIONS AND MEDITATIONS

1. The ministry of the Holy Spirit is to cleanse us, enlighten us, empower, and equip us for the continued ministry of Jesus Christ here on earth.
2. Do you merely possess, or have you allowed the Holy Spirit to empower you?

CHAPTER 9

"THE HOLY SPIRIT: EXHIBIT A"

"For as yet He had fallen upon none of them. They had only been baptized in the name of the Lord Jesus. Then they laid hands on them, and they received the Holy Spirit." (Acts 8:16, 17)

Throughout the history of Christianity, there has been some confusion as to what part the Holy Spirit plays in the matter of salvation. In the last chapter, we established some facts about The Holy Spirit:

- He is the third person of the Trinity: Father, Son, and Holy Spirit.
- He is a person not a force or thing having personality, will, intellect, and emotions.
- He is God and equal in every way with the Father and with the Son.
- He has come to convict the world of sin, righteousness, and judgment.
- He shows sinners that *Jesus is the way, the truth, and the life.*
- He hinders the growth of lawlessness.
- He regenerates us, we become "born again". (John 3:5)

- He comes to dwell within each of us at the time of salvation. (1 Corinthians 3:16; 1 Corinthians 6:19, 20; Romans 8:11)
- He seals each of us in Christ for that day of Redemption. (Ephesians 1:13; 4:30)
- He is the guarantee of salvation that each of us will one day receive. (2 Corinthians 5:5)
- He baptizes each of us into the Body of Christ. (1 Corinthians 12:13; Galatians 3:27; Romans 6:3, 4; Acts 1:5)
- He fills every yielded one of us for service. (Ephesians 5:18-20)

The problem arises as to how the relationship of being *filled* with the Holy Spirit relates to the matter of *salvation*.

There are three occasions in the book of Acts where speaking in tongues accompanied the receiving of the Holy Spirit: Acts 2:3-4, 10:46, 19:6. There are other passages, such as the one before us, where it is implied but not specifically declared, that authentic salvation must be accompanied by a physical manifestation of the Spirit—specifically speaking in tongues.

While there are *occasional* occurrences of this manifestation in Scripture, we must be careful in declaring the occasional *normative*. The greatest evidence of which is that the apostle Paul declares in 1 Corinthians 12:28, where a listing of gifts is found, and in Chapters 13 and 14. Paul provides an extended discussion on the matter of tongues, and declares that speaking in tongues is a gift that can be possessed by some but not all. It is not a premier gift, it is not above all others, and the one who possesses it needs to exercise care, in its use in the context of community.

This may be something of which you have had no concern, never thought about, but it needs to become a settled issue in your life for the Devil has used this to divide Christians throughout time.

In our text, we find the issue of tongues juxtaposed, that is placed side by side, with the matter of salvation, and we want to have some clarity on what is needful.

THE SEEMING NEED FOR SOMETHING MORE

"Now when the apostles who were at Jerusalem heard that Samaria had received the word of God, they sent Peter and John to them." (vs. 14)

Samaria was an important city for evangelizing. It was the Israelite capital city. It was a place where Jews had intermarried with Gentiles. We might say that it was a Gentile stronghold. In Acts 1:8 Luke specifically declares that Jesus said, *"But you shall receive power when the Holy Spirit has come upon you; and you shall be witnesses to Me in Jerusalem, and in all Judea and Samaria, and to the end of the earth."* In the situation of our text, Peter recently had delivered a stinging indictment for Christianity that resulted in 3,000 being saved, subsequent manifestations of healing through the hands of the apostles, the deaths of Ananias and Sapphira for lying to the Holy Spirit, and the martyrdom of Stephen. Therefore, the expectation was that a great manifestation of the Holy Spirit would occur at this important city.

Being a Gentile stronghold, it was important that there was more than verbal acknowledgement of the matter of salvation. The apostles desired to see real evidence that had been seen at Jerusalem. They desired something more. Therefore, they sent for Peter and John, the spiritual leadership to certify, to validate the true Gentile's conversion.

In our religious persuasion, in our churches, we see some who will confess Christ as Lord and Savior; where later there is no outward evidence of true conversion. Whether a person speaks or does not speak in tongues is no evidence of real conversion. Biblically, we are not called to assess a person's salvation by any other means than their confession of faith and inspecting the fruit of their life. In the physical realm, we say, if it barks like a dog, quacks like a duck, moos like a cow, we can assume it to be what it is. In the spiritual realm, if a person has been saved, there ought to be evidence consist with the claim. Ultimately, only God knows a person's heart, and we can only compare their testimony with what fruit they bear.

THE MANIFESTATION

> *". . . who, when they had come down, prayed for them that they might receive the Holy Spirit. For as yet He had fallen upon none of them. They had only been baptized in the name of the Lord Jesus."* (vs. 15-16)

The text informs us that there was a desire for them to see, for something to occur, beyond the matter of baptism. After all, wasn't this something that John the Baptist had declared needful at the beginning of Jesus ministry.

John the Baptist spoke to those being baptized in Mark 1:8 saying, *"I indeed baptized you with water, but He* (meaning Jesus) *will baptize you with the Holy Spirit."* That baptism occurred among the disciples on the day of Pentecost where 3,000 were saved. The question is, was that *normative* for us, is it *prescriptive* for salvation? Evidently, those who sent Peter and John to Samaria thought it *normative* and they came and prayed for them to receive the Holy Spirit.

Although it is not specifically declared here in our text, the manifestation of tongues is implied. Verses 17-19 records, *"Then they laid hands on them, and they received the Holy Spirit. And when Simon saw that through the laying on of the apostles' hands the Holy Spirit was given, he offered them money, saying, "Give me this power also, that anyone on whom I lay hands may receive the Holy Spirit."* (vs. 17-19)

Simon, which 8: 9 tells us before his conversion *"previously practiced sorcery in the city and astonished the people of Samaria, claiming that he was someone great,"* was a witness to what happened and desired to have this ability as well. Although not specifically stated, we can assume what he saw was the physical manifestation of speaking in tongues.

Historically, those of Pentecostal and Holiness persuasions most often associate the gift of speaking in tongues, glossalia, or what are called ecstatic languages, as evidence of the manifestation of the Holy Spirit and of being filled with the Spirit.

Some go as far to propose that there is what is called a "second blessing." This becomes the point of contention. Is there a need for what is called the "second blessing?" That is, something beyond a confession of faith. Something beyond being baptized to occur for a person to be saved, or to be filled with the Holy Spirit?

There are those who propose that one is not really saved unless they speak in tongues, because that is the model that we see in Scripture. They contend it is one thing to come into the saving knowledge of Jesus Christ, be born again, and baptized into the body of Christ. However, it is totally another thing to be filled with the spirit, the evidence being of speaking in tongues. On this basis, salvation is of two parts: baptism in water, and baptism in the Holy Spirit.

Some in our society are stuck on a denominational label: Baptist, Methodist, Catholic, Lutheran, etc., and limit what spiritual gifts they exercise in the community of church accordingly. All those labels help people to recognize and identify to some extent how worship is conducted within the sanctuary walls and some foundational beliefs.

Our religious persuasion ought not and should not define what is allowable. Rather, if it is prescribed or allowed in the Bible it is available. If it is biblical and exercised in accordance with Scripture—that is, done decently and in order, it is allowable. We are first biblical and second, we are believers.

As related to salvation, salvation is a matter of confessing Christ as Lord and Savior (Romans 10:9-10, 13). There is nothing we can do to merit salvation (Ephesians 2:8, 9; Titus 3:5). We are saved by God's grace. Once you are saved, you are always saved (2 Corinthians 1:21, 22; Ephesians 1:13, 14). We do not fall in and out of being saved, based on our behavior. Salvation is a matter of our position in and through Christ and not our daily practice. The variable is whether or not a person is truly saved. The standard is a person's confession of faith, and the subsequent fruit that they bear. It is not a matter of speaking in tongues or not.

However, ultimately it is not for us to decide, but up to God. It is a matter of the heart. On the Day of Judgment, many whom we thought were *out*, will make it *in*; and many that we thought were *in* will be left *out*.

WHY TONGUES?

Paul tells us in 1 Corinthians 14:1, 2 to desire spiritual gifts, several which are listed in 1 Corinthians 12:4-13, not only tongues. In 1 Corinthians 14:1 Paul says, *"Pursue love, and desire spiritual gifts, but especially that you may prophesy."* Paul says it is more needful for us to prophesy, not in the sense of being a prophet, but in the sense of sharing the gospel that others might be saved. So why tongues?

Some would say that tongues are a gift for personal edification. Paul says in 1 Corinthians 14:2-4, *"For he who speaks in a tongue does not speak to men but to God, for no one understands him; however, in the spirit he speaks mysteries. But he who prophesies speaks edification and exhortation and comfort to men. He who speaks in a tongue edifies himself, but he who prophesies edifies the church."* Again, in 1 Corinthians 14:5 Paul says, *"I wish you all spoke with tongues, but even more that you prophesied; for he who prophesies is greater than he who speaks with tongues, unless indeed he interprets, that the church may receive edification."* Although some sort of personal edification can occur, for Paul it was about the edification of the church, not just the individual.

Some would say it is a spiritual aid in the matter of prayer. Romans 8:26-27 declares, *"Likewise the Spirit also helps in our weaknesses. For we do not know what we should pray for as we ought, but the Spirit Himself makes intercession for us with groanings which cannot be uttered. Now He who searches the hearts knows what the mind of the Spirit is, because He makes intercession for the saints according to the will of God."* However, the Holy Spirit does that for us all, whether we speak in tongues or not, but possibly in some way the connection is different. I don't know, the Bible is silent; all I know is what Paul has to say about it. In 1 Corinthians 14:14 he says, *"For if I pray in a tongue, my spirit prays, but my understanding is unfruitful."*

Speaking and praying in tongues is most definitely an issue on which Christians can respectfully and lovingly agree to disagree. Praying in tongues is not what determines salvation. Speaking and praying in tongues is not what separates a mature Christian from an immature Christian. Whether there is such a thing as praying in tongues as a personal prayer language is not a fundamental of the Christian faith. Therefore, whether we believe in speaking or praying in tongues as a private prayer language for personal edification or not, we recognize that many who practice such are our brothers and sisters in Christ and are worthy of our love and respect.

A WORD OF WARNING

"And when Simon saw that through the laying on of the apostles' hands the Holy Spirit was given, he offered them money, saying, "Give me this power also, that anyone on whom I lay hands may receive the Holy Spirit." But Peter said to him, "Your money perish with you, because you thought that the gift of God could be purchased with money!" (Acts 8:18-20)

When Simon saw, the apostles lay hands on people and they began to speak with tongues, he was impressed and desirous of this ability as well. As we find in the text, it was not because he wanted to use it for spiritual purposes, but because he wanted to advance his standing in the community. Again, Acts 8:9 tells us of him, *"But there was a certain man called Simon, who previously practiced sorcery in the city and astonished the people of Samaria, claiming that he was someone great.*"

Unfortunately, there are still Simons in our society of the saved, who put forth the matter of speaking in tongues to elevate themselves somehow as super Christians. To promote themselves as possessing something that others do not have, and that they are therefore more spiritual, more in tune with God and the things of God. As with Simon, they desire to astonish the people and set themselves up as someone great.

Paul tells us to desire spiritual gifts (1 Corinthians 14:1, 5). If you desire to speak in tongues, make sure that it's not about exalting you. It is only one of the spiritual gifts that God has made available to us. It is more outwardly visible, and peculiar, than some of the other gifts. However, 1 Corinthians 12:8-10 tells us, *"The manifestation of the Spirit is given to each one for the profit of all: for to one is given the word of wisdom through the Spirit, to another the word of knowledge through the same Spirit, to another faith by the same Spirit, to another gifts of healings by the same Spirit, to another the working of miracles, to another prophecy, to another discerning of spirits, to another different kinds of tongues, to another the interpretation of tongues."* Verse 11 grounds us in the fact that it is not about us, but *"one and the same Spirit works all these things, distributing to each one individually as He wills."*

You might say, "So? How does this apply to me?" All God's spiritual gifts are given to people in the church as a means of equipping people to do the work of ministry that builds up the body of Christ to help us all to arrive at maturity and completeness. A spiritual gift is something, spiritual in nature, which can be done with ease and effectiveness. They are not just for our selfish use but they work together for the common good of all of us. 1 Peter 4:10, 11 says, *"Each one should use whatever gift he has received to serve others faithfully administering God's grace in its various forms. If anyone speaks, he should do it as one speaking the very words of God. If anyone serves, he should do it with the strength God provides so that in all things God may be praised through Jesus Christ."* Whatever spiritual gift we may have we can be assured that God has given it to us though the Holy Spirit for the edifying of the body of Christ.

****

Throughout the book of Acts, thousands of people believe in Jesus and nothing is said about them speaking in tongues (Acts 2:41, 8:5-25, 16:31-34, 21:20). Nowhere in the New Testament is it taught that speaking in tongues is the only evidence a person has received the Holy Spirit. In fact, the New Testament teaches the opposite. We are told that every believer in Christ has the Holy Spirit (Romans 8:9; 1 Corinthians 12:13; Ephesians 1:13-14), but not every believer speaks in tongues (1 Corinthians 12:29-31).

Just because a person speaks in tongues does not make them more spiritual than another person. It does not establish their connection to God as being more secure than another's. The standard by which God recognizes our commitment of faith and responds to our faith is the matter of obedience to His Word. Always has been and always will be.

If the purpose of the gifts is to build up the church and equip it to become mature and complete, then each of us have a responsibility to find out in what ways we have been gifted so that we will become a productive part of the body of Christ. We help to build up others and at the same time, they help to build us up.

REFLECTIONS AND MEDITATIONS

1. Speaking in tongues is not essential for salvation.
2. What spiritual gifts have you discovered that you possess?

CHAPTER 10

"GOD HAS SEALED US"

"who also has sealed us and given us the Spirit in our hearts as a guarantee." (2 Corinthians 1:22)

We all remember the problems that were experienced in the past with product tampering, such as with Tylenol back in 1982. These occurrences led manufacturers to place seals upon their products. Statements such as, "quality ensured if seal is intact" are common place on just about everything we buy, particularly medicines. The seal ensures that the product inside is good. It is sealed at the factory to protect it until it comes to its goal of providing you, the recipient, with the relief of pain, or hunger, or whatever.

There is a seal placed on every believer at the time of our regeneration. Assuring each believer that no one has tampered with his or her salvation, certifying each believer to be, eternally secure. The words of our text, 2 Corinthians 1:21, 22 tells us, *"Now He who establishes us with you in Christ and has anointed us is God, who also has sealed us and given us the Spirit in our hearts as a guarantee."*

Each of person who believes has been sealed. The moment we trusted Christ as our Savior, God sealed us. Considering the varied use of this term, several questions must be addressed:

1. What is the nature of this seal? Are we sealed like a letter? Are we sealed like a tomb? Branded like cattle, or horses?
2. What is the purpose of our sealing?
3. How long are we sealed?

WHAT IS THE NATURE OF THIS SEAL?

The term sealed is used various ways in the New Testament. In Matthew 27:66, we read that Jesus' tomb was sealed by the Romans. In Revelation 20, we are told that Satan was bound and sealed in the bottomless pit for one thousand years. In Revelation 6 there are several references to books that were sealed. In Revelation 7, we read that during the tribulation God will place a seal on 144,000 people from the tribe of Israel.

In every case the term sealed carried with it the ideas of protection and security. To seal something whether it was a document or tomb was to close it off from outside influences and interferences.

That is still true today. We seal windows and doors to keep out the wind. We seal letters to keep everyone out except the recipient. We seal our basements to keep out water. We even put a seal on our furniture to keep the dust from getting into the pores of the wood and fabric.

As a believer, you have been sealed. The Sealer is God, not the Holy Spirit; for it is said, *"Now He who establishes us with you in Christ and has anointed us is God, who also has sealed us and given us the Spirit in our hearts as a guarantee"* (2 Corinthians 1:21, 22). The seal is not baptism, or the Lord's Supper, or some extraordinary gifts, but the Holy Spirit Himself.

It is the believers that are sealed. It is not truths, or promises, or experiences that are sealed upon the heart; it is believers themselves who are sealed. A hard, cold, lifeless heart cannot receive the seal.

The condition on which Christians are sealed is by faith. As a preliminary, the gospel must be heard, but all who hear are not sealed. We must individually and voluntarily yield submission to the truth we have received.

The true seal authenticates us to ourselves. Romans 8:16 tells us, *"The Spirit Himself bears witness with our spirit that we are children of God."*

WHAT IS THE PURPOSE OF OUR SEALING?

In our culture, we do not usually think of putting a seal on people. Cattle and horses are branded or a seal of ownership placed upon them, but humans to our way of thinking are not. Therefore, it is a bit difficult to imagine the significance of being sealed by God. Fortunately, we have an illustration in Scripture that clarifies this matter for us.

Revelation 7:4 tells us, during the Tribulation God will place a seal on 144,000 Jews, *"And I heard the number of those who were sealed. One hundred and forty-four thousand of all the tribes of the children of Israel were sealed."* Whoever the 144,000 are the seal is apparently some sort of visible mark on the forehead. As the Tribulation progresses, it becomes evident that the members of this group bearing God's seal have been granted supernatural protection from the chaos surrounding them. At the end of the Tribulation period, the entire group reappears to welcome the King. Revelation 14:1-3 tells us, *"Then I looked, and behold, a Lamb standing on Mount Zion, and with Him one hundred and forty-four thousand, having His Father's name written on their foreheads. And I heard a voice from heaven, like the voice of many waters, and like the voice of loud thunder. And I heard the sound of harpists playing their harps. They sang as it were a new song before the throne, before the four living creatures, and the elders; and no one could learn that song except the hundred and forty-four thousand who were redeemed from the earth."*

This powerful illustration helps us to understand the ramifications of God's placing His Seal on an individual. The primary benefit of the seal is that of protection. The seal protects this group during the most dangerous period in the history of humanity. Nothing can overcome the power of this seal. Not even the Antichrist himself!

Unlike the 144,000 mentioned in Revelation, our seal is not visible. We have been sealed *"in Him."* Our seal is spiritual, not physical. Instead of receiving a mark on our foreheads, we were given the Holy Spirit as a pledge of God's intent to preserve us. The Holy Spirit is a pledge of God's intentions. He is not finished with us yet, but the presence of the Spirit demonstrates God's commitment to complete what He has started. If salvation is not permanent God is simply playing games by sending the Spirit into our hearts. It would be as a man giving a woman an engagement ring when he knows he has no intention of marrying her.

The device used to indicate God's seal in our lives is certainly different from the one He chose for the 144,000. His purpose for sealing us, however, is the same. Just as their physical seal protected them from losing physical life, so our spiritual seal ensures the longevity of spiritual life. Just as the physical forces of evil could not take away the physical life of those Jews who bore the seal, so, too, the spiritual forces of darkness cannot put an end to the spiritual life of God's people.

The shepherd has some mark that he places on each of his sheep, so that if any of them strays away it may at once be known as his. Even so Christ, the good Shepherd, has a mark by which He knows, and would have all know, the members of His flock. The mark is the seal of the Spirit. God stamps His people by giving them His presence.

2 Timothy 2:19 tells us in part that *". . . the Lord knows those who are His."*

John 10:14 tells us, *"I am the good shepherd; and I know My sheep, and am known by My own."*

1 Corinthians 6:19, 20 tells us, *"Or do you not know that your body is the temple of the Holy Spirit who is in you, whom you have from God, and you are not your own? For you were bought at a price; therefore glorify God in your body and in your spirit, which are God's."*

HOW LONG DOES THE SEAL LAST?

"…and given us the Spirit in our hearts"

God does infinitely more than just save us. Romans 8:32 tells us that God has given unto us a multitude of other blessings as well. *"He who did not spare His own Son, but delivered Him up for us all, how shall He not with Him also freely give us all things?"* The Holy Spirit is the first of God's gifts to the obedient believer in Christ, and so becomes the assurance of all promised blessings to come.

In present-day transactions "earnest money" is a part of the agreed price, a down payment, indicating the buyers pledge to pay the rest in due time. The Holy Spirit is the title deed, the guarantee to our future inheritance, the seed from which will spring the flower of an immortal life.

The earnest is more than a guarantee. It is small in comparison with the full payment, but it is a partial payment which binds the bargain and obliges both the buyer and seller to complete the transaction. The gift of the Holy Spirit is the first instalment, as it were, of the infinite treasure that God plans to bestow upon us. It is the guarantee of the final entry into possession of the whole inheritance the Father has reserved for His children.

Paul said it this way in Ephesians 1:13, 14, *"In Him you also trusted, after you heard the word of truth, the gospel of your salvation; in whom also, having believed, you were sealed with the Holy Spirit of promise, who is the guarantee of our inheritance until the redemption of the purchased possession, to the praise of His glory."*

How long does the seal last? As long as the 144,000 bear the seal, they will be safe. If we are sealed in Him, we are safe as well. God has been gracious to give us an answer through the apostle Paul as found in Ephesians 4:30, *"And do not grieve the Holy Spirit of God, by whom you were sealed for the day of redemption."* We are sealed right through the *"day of redemption."* The day of redemption refers to the day when our salvation will be complete—body and spirit--until that day and no day short of that.

Those of you who "can" are familiar with the process of purifying your jars, filling them with food, and then sealing. As long as that seal remains intact the quality of the food canned is preserved.

First Peter 1:3, 4 tells us, *"Blessed be the God and Father of our Lord Jesus Christ, who according to His abundant mercy has begotten us again to a living hope through the resurrection of Jesus Christ from the dead, to an inheritance incorruptible and undefiled and that does not fade away, reserved in heaven for you."* Our salvation is imperishable, undefiled, and unfading. You might say that we have been purified and sealed. If that seal is intact the contents are ensured. Things may get dirty on the outside but if that seal is intact the contents are preserved.

There are no exceptions. Everyone who has been sealed in Christ will remain sealed up through the end. Peter echoes this thought in his first epistle, 1 Peter 1:5. He points out that each believer has an inheritance reserved in heaven. Believers, he says, *"who are kept by the power of God through faith for salvation ready to be revealed in the last time"*

Again, we find that our salvation will not be complete until the end of time. But until then, we are kept, we are protected by *"the power of God."*

The seal is a security. All the authority of its owner, all the authority of God, accompanies it. Christian being once owned will never be deserted by God.

A security that may be broken at any time, or the value of which depends upon man's ability to remain faithful, or on man's own good works, is no security at all. The word tells us our security will last beyond death: *"till the day of redemption."* The apostle never regards the day of death as marking the day of final security. Rather he fixes it for that day that completes the redemption in the re-joining of body and soul in their changeless incorruptibility.

Our salvation will not be complete until we receive our new bodies. *"For this corruptible must put on incorruption, and this mortal must put on immortality."* (1 Corinthians 15:53)

As it is stated in the book of Romans 8:23 *". . . we ourselves groan within ourselves, eagerly waiting for the adoption, the redemption of our body."* Here in this world we are incognito; we are not recognized as the sons of God, but someday we shall throw off this disguise. First John 3:2 tells us, *"It has not yet been revealed what we shall be, but we know that when He is revealed, we shall be like Him, for we shall see Him as He is."* The full revelation of the sons of God is reserved for a future day.

Revelation 5:1-5 tells us, *"And I saw in the right hand of Him who sat on the throne a scroll written inside and on the back, sealed with seven seals. Then I saw a strong angel proclaiming with a loud voice, "Who is worthy to open the scroll and to loose its seals?" And no one in heaven or on the earth or under the earth was able to open the scroll, or to look at it. So I wept much, because no one was found worthy to open and read the scroll, or to look at it. But one of the elders said to me, "Do not weep. Behold, the Lion of the tribe of Judah, the Root of David, has prevailed to open the scroll and to loose its seven seals."*

****

The renowned preacher and expositor, Charles Spurgeon, published a small devotional book entitled, "A Check Book of the Bank of Faith." It provided a short devotional message and a promise from the Word of God for each day of the year. Spurgeon commented that each promise was as good as money in the bank to anyone who would claim it by faith. It was as simple as writing a check against God's unlimited bank account.

Jesus had promised the coming of the Holy Spirit, and on the Day of Pentecost Peter told his hearers that those who repented and were baptized would receive the gift of the Holy Spirit. The Spirit's indwelling gives the believers in Christ assurance of salvation. Paul refers to the "Holy Spirit of promise, who is the guarantee of our inheritance." The Spirit has given to us as a deposit guaranteeing that we shall one day receive the full inheritance God has for us. You can count on it like money in the bank. Well, it's more certain than that!

The scriptures clearly teach that God has already sealed us and has determined to leave the seal intact until our salvation is complete. How, then, could we possibly lose our salvation? To be unsaved, or unadopted children of God, would mean to remove the seal. Who could possibly do that? Our worthiness did not get us sealed, neither did our works nor good looks. It was God's gift of grace despite everything we were.

For those who maintain that salvation is not forever, this question poses an insurmountable obstacle. For those who believe otherwise, it leaves us with unquestionable certainty, with the confidence in an eternal security.

We can be assured, according to the Word, if God has marked us for His own, none shall pluck us out of His hand. Though the universe should rise up against a sealed saint, it should ingloriously fail; for the Divine seal is the pledge that an Omnipotent God will defend the seal.

REFLECTIONS AND MEDITATIONS

1. We are sealed until God decides to take us to be with Him.

CHAPTER 11

"WHO THEN IS GOING TO HELL?"

"For God so loved the world that he gave His only begotten Son, that whosoever believeth in Him should not perish, but have everlasting life." (John 3:16)

Eternal damnation is undoubtedly one of the most difficult, if not the most difficult, teachings of the Christian faith. How can God justify punishing a man or woman eternally for sins committed over a period of a few years? It doesn't seem right. Yet the Scriptures teach that Hell is a real place for real people. Revelation 20:10, 15 declares, *"The devil, who deceived them, was cast into the lake of fire and brimstone where the beast and the false prophet are. And they will be tormented day and night forever and ever... And anyone not found written in the Book of Life was cast into the lake of fire."*

In the minds of many there are certain sins so grave that God either cannot or will not forgive them. Consequently, those who have involved themselves in these actions are destined for Hell.

If that were the case, surely God would have led someone to record for us in the Bible a list of the unpardonable sins. A loving God would not leave us to guess about such a vital issue. But that kind of list does not exist. In 1 Corinthians 6:9-11 Paul lists a variety of sin but concludes that those who have committed such sin have been forgiven, *"Do you not know that the unrighteous will not inherit the kingdom of God? Do not be deceived. Neither fornicators, nor idolaters, nor adulterers, nor homosexuals, nor sodomites, nor thieves, nor covetous, nor drunkards, nor revilers, nor extortioners will inherit the kingdom of God. And such were some of you. But you were washed, but you were sanctified, but you were justified in the name of the Lord Jesus and by the Spirit of our God."*

People of all manner of sexual and unethical sins have found forgiveness through Christ. Hell, is not reserved for those who commit certain types of sin.

If there are sins so severe that they determine a person's fate, certainly the murder of the Son of God would be one. What greater crime could be committed in the whole of human history? Yet, in the gospel of Luke we read that Jesus looked down on the very people who were crucifying Him and said, *"Father, forgive them, for they do not know what they do"* (Luke 23:34). As strange as it may sound, killing the Son of God was not severe enough to put those men outside the boundaries of God's offer of forgiveness.

How does all this relate to the subject of eternal security? The debate is over whether a man can be on his way to heaven one minute and on his way to Hell the next. To answer that question, we must understand exactly what sends a person to Hell, i.e. can we flip-flop between heaven and Hell? Heaven will be full of people who committed all kinds of sin. It takes more than simply sinning to get to Hell.

What then sends a person to Hell? What guarantees the omission of a man's or woman's name from the book of life? What is the ingredient that, mixed with sins, somehow ensures one condemnation to the Lake of Fire? Sinning alone will not do, for as we have seen, sinners of every description have the potential for escaping Hell. We will find answers to these questions as we consider the following:

1. Who then is going to Hell?
2. What about those who stop believing?
3. God's faithfulness

WHO THEN IS GOING TO HELL?

The clearest teaching on this subject is conveyed in the conversation between Jesus and Nicodemus. It is a passage that contains what may be the most familiar verse in the entire New Testament:

"For God so loved the world that He gave His only begotten Son, that whoever believes in Him should not perish but have everlasting life. For God did not send His Son into the world to condemn the world, but that the world through Him might be saved." (John 3:16, 17)

What keeps a person from perishing? What keeps a person from an eternal damnation? Jesus did not cite for Nicodemus a list of sins and then add, "As long as a man keeps himself from these, he will not perish." His only condition was belief in Him.

Notice His next words; *"He who believes in Him is not condemned; but he who does not believe is condemned already, because he has not believed in the name of the only begotten Son of God."* (vs. 18)

Look at this verse and answer this question: According to Jesus, what must a person do to keep from being judged for sin? Must he stop doing something? Must he promise to stop doing something? The answer is so simple that many stumble over it without even seeing it. All Jesus requires is that the individual *"believe on Him."*

Look again. What is true of someone who has already been judged? Did he commit an unpardonable sin of some sort? No! He is judged because he has *"not believed in"* the Son of God.

Sinners who do not put their trust in Christ perish and miss eternal life. In fact, sinners who reject Christ have done it to themselves; they are as good as there! They would have nothing to do with Christ in this life, and so they shall have nothing to do with Him in eternity. It is not lying, cheating, stealing, raping, murdering, or being unfaithful that sends people to Hell. It is rejecting Christ, refusing to put their trust in Him for the forgiveness of sin.

Jesus message was simple. Eternal life is found through faith and faith alone. Both heaven and Hell will be full of men and women who have committed every imaginable evil. The difference is not in the severity of their sin, or in the number of their offenses, but in their response to the offer of the Savior.

BUT WHAT ABOUT THOSE WHO STOP BELIEVING?

Some people argue that the believer must maintain their faith to maintain their salvation. If our salvation is gained through believing in Christ, doesn't it make sense that salvation would be lost if we quit believing? The primary scriptural support for this view comes from the apostle John's use of the present tense in connection with the term believe, to denote continuous, uninterrupted action. In other words, they understand John 3:16 to read, *"That whoever believes in Him should not perish but have everlasting life."* The implication is that *"whoever does not keep on believing will not have eternal life"* or *"will lose eternal life."*

When a man or woman believes, he or she is given eternal life-right then and there. It is a gift. Ephesians 2:8, 9 declares, *"For by grace you have been saved through faith, and that not of yourselves; it is the gift of God, not of works, lest anyone should boast."* At that moment in time the transaction is completed.

A gift that can be taken back is no gift. True gifts have no strings attached. Once you place a condition of any kind on a gift, it becomes a trade, not a gift. In the case of salvation God has a strict no-return policy. There is no evidence by way of statement or illustration that God has ever taken back from a believer the gift of salvation once it has been given. His love would keep Him from doing so. Keep in mind, Christ came to seek and to save the lost. Why would He take back what He came to give?

We are not saved by our faith. We are saved by grace. The instrument of salvation was and is grace. God came up with a plan and carried it out through Christ. We did not take part in it, nor did we deserve any part of it.

Faith does not save a person. Everybody has expressed faith at some point or another. Yet not everyone will spend eternity in heaven. God's grace is what saves us. Our faith, however, is the thing that bridges the gap between our need and God's provision; specifically, it is a point at which the expression of faith in Christ brings God's provision of grace together with our need.

Faith is simply the way we say yes to God's free gift of eternal life. Faith and salvation are not one and the same any more than a gift and the hand that receives it are the same. Salvation or justification or adoption-whatever you wish to call it-stands independently of faith. Consequently, God does not require a constant attitude of faith to be saved-only an act of faith.

An illustration may be helpful. If I chose to have a tattoo put on my arm that would involve a one-time act on my part. Yet the tattoo would remain with me indefinitely. I don't have to maintain an attitude of fondness for tattoos to ensure that the tattoo remains on my arm. In fact, I may change my mind the minute I receive it. But that does not change the fact that I have a tattoo on my arm. My request for the tattoo and the tattoo itself are two entirely different things. I received it by asking and paying for it. But asking for my money back and changing my attitude will not undo what was done.

God's forgiveness and salvation is applied the moment of faith. It is not the same thing as faith. And its permanence is not contingent upon the permanence of one's faith. You and I are not saved because we have enduring faith. We are saved because at a moment in time we expressed faith in our enduring Lord.

Faith is our way of accepting God's gift. Faith serves as our spiritual hands by which the gift is received at a moment in time. Again, saving faith is not necessarily a sustained attitude of gratefulness for God's gift. It is a singular moment in time wherein we take what God has offered.

All of us have periods of doubt. That is to be expected because Satan and his gangs are constantly at work trying to destroy our faith. Just as he has an occasional victory in other areas of our lives, so he is likely to have an occasional victory in this area as well.

We are in a war. It's a war we will ultimately win, but it's a war in which there are real casualties. How comforting it is to know that though the enemy may temporarily steal our victory, he cannot touch our salvation. Having done nothing to earn it, we can do nothing to lose it!

AN ILLUSTRATION OF GOD'S FAITHFULNESS.

Does the Scripture teach that regardless of the consistency of our faith, our salvation is secure: Yes, it does, through both proposition and illustration as found in 2 Timothy 2:11-13:

"This is a faithful saying:
For if we died with Him,
We shall also live with Him.
If we endure,
We shall also reign with Him.
If we deny Him,
He also will deny us.
If we are faithless,
He remains faithful;
He cannot deny Himself.

This one passage highlights four basic doctrines.

1. First, all believers have the potential to experience the abundant life.
2. Second, faithful believers will be rewarded for their faithfulness.
3. Third, unfaithful believers will be denied the recognition that would have been theirs if they had remained faithful.
4. And last, believers who lose or abandon their faith will retain their salvation for God remains faithful.

Christ will not deny an unbelieving Christian his or her salvation because to do so would be to deny Himself. Why?

Faithful, or not, every person who has at any time had saving faith is a permanent part of the body of Christ. Whatever action Christ takes against a believer, He takes against Himself, for each believer is a part of His body.

The unfaithful believer will not receive a special place in the kingdom of Christ like those who are fortunate enough to be allowed to reign with Him. But the unfaithful believer will not lose his salvation.

The apostle Paul must have known this concept is difficult to accept. The Holy Son of God allowing a person to retain their salvation once they have lost their faith? That is not an easy pill to swallow. To his credit, Paul included the reason Christ will not take back His gift of eternal life: *"He cannot deny Himself."* Paul is alluding to the union each believer shares in the body of Christ. Once a person places trust in Christ's death as the payment for sin, they immediately become part of the body of Christ.

The Bible not only states that our salvation is secure despite our faithlessness but illustrates this truth as well. The weakness of these illustrations, however, is that they argue from silence. In these instances, the Bible never actually says, *"Even though he lost his faith, he did not lose his salvation."* But neither does the text assert that a person or group abandoned the faith and thus lost salvation. Thus, readers are left to decide for themselves.

The strength of this argument lies in the fact that there are several individuals in scripture who stopped believing for a time and yet their salvation is never questioned. Even during the period in which their faith wavered, their eternal security is never debated.

If salvation is contingent on the continuity of faith, these narratives would have been the perfect places to set forth this significant bit of theology. Yet, as we will see, these portions of Scripture are used to confirm the very opposite view. In each case, we find that God remains faithful, even to the faithless.

The apostle Peter provides an excellent illustration of the verses we examined in 2 Timothy. We know that Peter was a believer. When Christ asked Peter who he thought He was, Peter answered. *"You are the Christ, the Son of the living God"* (Matthew 16:16)."

And Jesus responded, *"Blessed are you, Simon Bar-Jonah, for flesh and blood has not revealed this to you, but My Father who is in heaven. And I also say to you that you are Peter, and on this rock I will build My church, and the gates of Hades shall not prevail against it."* (Matthew 16:17, 18)

Peter had the correct answer to Jesus' question, and Jesus responded by promising to include him in the founding of the church.

On another occasion, Jesus asked the Twelve if they would abandon Him as many of His other followers had begun to do (John 6:6, 7). Once again Peter's answer reveals his faith in the Savior. *"But Simon Peter answered Him, "Lord, to whom shall we go? You have the words of eternal life. Also we have come to believe and know that You are the Christ, the Son of the living God."* (John 6:68-69)

Peter was a believer all right, but his faith was not unshakable. And Jesus knew it. On the night of His arrest. Jesus broke the news to Peter, *"And the Lord said, Simon, Simon, behold, Satan hath desire to have you, that he may sift you as wheat . . ."* (Luke 22:31). Then Jesus said, *"But I have prayed for you, that your faith should not fail; and when you have returned to Me, strengthen your brethren"* (Luke 22:32). Satan's attack would center on Peter's faith. Jesus anticipated that. And He anticipated Peter's temporary defeat as well. But nowhere did Peter's salvation come into question.

Think about it. Jesus acknowledged that Peter was going to turn away from Him; that he would deny Him publicly at the most crucial time in His earthly life; and that his faith would be dealt a severe blow. Yet His final words to Peter were words of comfort. Peter was about to enter a time in which his faith would be in jeopardy-but not his salvation. Even though Peter would be faithless, Christ remained faithful.

****

We have heard it a thousand times: *"Be sober, be vigilant; because your adversary the devil walks about like a roaring lion, seeking whom he may devour."* (1 Peter 5:8)

But have you ever wondered what the enemy is seeking to devour? The next verse tells us; *"Resist him, steadfast in the faith."* (1 Peter 5:9)

Satan wants to destroy your faith. Once that is weakened or gone altogether, you are powerless against him. Your confidence is gone, and for all practical purposes you are useless to the kingdom of God.

Our faith is constantly under attack. Some battles we will win, some we will lose. At times, we will feel as if we could move mountains. At other times, we will find ourselves crying out to God for a sign. But regardless of the shape our faith is in, our salvation is always intact. For whereas our faith is often turned into our changing circumstances, our salvation is anchored in the unchanging nature and grace of God.

The Bible clearly teaches that God's love for His people is of such a magnitude that even those who walk away from the faith have not the slightest chance of slipping from His hand. Faith is not the reason God saves us. Love is the reason.

"For God so loved the world that He gave His only begotten Son, that whoever believes in Him should not perish but have everlasting life."

Ephesians 2:4-7 further declares, *"But God, who is rich in mercy, because of His great love with which He loved us, even when we were dead in trespasses, made us alive together with Christ (by grace you have been saved), and raised us up together, and made us sit together in the heavenly places in Christ Jesus, that in the ages to come He might show the exceeding riches of His grace in His kindness toward us in Christ Jesus."*

REFLECTIONS AND MEDITATIONS

1. Only those who refuse to believe will suffer an eternal damnation. All others, regardless of the nature of their sin can be saved.

CHAPTER 12

"DOES WHAT WE DO REALLY MATTER?"

"Each one's work will become clear; for the Day will declare it, because it will be revealed by fire; and the fire will test each one's work, of what sort it is." (1 Corinthians 3:13)

When we consider God's unconditional love and grace. When we come to the realization that people can trust Christ as their Savior and then for a season turn around and live any way that they please and still go to heaven; we are logically left with a bad taste in our mouths. The very idea makes the doctrine of eternal security seem totally unfair and unjust to those of us who are faithfully serving God. With this in mind, we must ask ourselves.

- Does the doctrine of eternal security allow people to "get by" with their sin?
- Can they get both the benefit of heaven and the pleasure of sin?
- If our salvation is secure, what reason is there to remain faithful?
- What do we say to persons who sincerely believe Christ died for them but have no use for holy living?
- Do Christians, in fact, get by with their sin?

Many persons who hold to eternal security respond to this dilemma by doubting the genuineness of the person's salvation who would even consider such a response to God's grace. In other words, a real Christian will obey Christ. Anyone who would use God's grace as an excuse to sin is not a Christian at all, they are not really saved.

Yet, the New Testament is full of exhortations against sin. In every case these are addressed to believers. If real Christians don't or can't abuse God's grace by getting involved with sin, why warn them against it? Obviously, the New Testament writers realized that Christians are as capable of sinning as the most lost of the lost.

Anyone who believes that a believer's sins carry no eternal consequences has overlooked a major area of biblical theology. Yet many believers think just that. Somewhere along the way they were taught or just assumed that heaven will be the same for everybody. If they are in, that is the only thing that matters. If heaven is going to be the same for everyone:

- There are no long-term consequences for not following God, why not partake from time to time of the pleasures of sin?
- Apart from appreciation for all God has done, is there any reason to be good?
- Do we have anything to lose by sinning?
- Is there anything to gain by staying pure?

We can have the best of both worlds!

The answers to these questions become evident when a person understands the Bible's teachings on man's ultimate destiny. In most cases, individuals who are genuinely disturbed by these questions have been misinformed about two things:

1. Where will Christians will spend eternity?
2. Will what we do then have anything to do with what we are doing now?

3. A biblical illustration.

WHERE WILL CHRISTIANS SPEND ETERNITY?

Most Christians have been taught to believe their ultimate destiny is heaven. That is not totally true. Man's ultimate destiny, according to Revelation 21:1, 3 is to dwell with God in a new heaven and in a new earth, *"And I saw a new heaven and a new earth: for the first heaven and the first earth were passed away: and there was no more sea . . . And I heard a voice out of heaven saying, behold the tabernacle of God is with men, and He will dwell with them, and they shall be His people, and God Himself shall be with them, and be their God."*

When God created the heavens and the earth, He intentionally placed humankind on the earth. He could have put us in heaven. But God placed humankind here for a specific purpose; to rule over creation (Genesis 1:28-31). The earth became our responsibility. To make His job easier, God designed a body for us that is tailor-made for living and working on planet earth.

That was God's plan in the beginning, and nowhere in Scripture are we informed that His original plan has been altered. On the contrary, all of Scripture teaches that we are moving toward a time in which God's original plan will be fulfilled. Part of the glorification of humankind will be the provision of a perfect environment in which to dwell.

When sin entered the world, death was close behind (Romans 5:12). Death was not a part of God's original plan for humankind. And eventually it will be done away with completely (1 Corinthians 15:54-56). In the meantime, however, death is a present reality.

When a believer dies, he or she goes immediately to be with the Lord (2 Corinthians 5:6-8). Since we know from numerous passages that Christ is seated at the right hand of God in heaven, it is safe to say that Christians go to heaven when they die (Colossians 3:1). Paul confirms this idea in his first letter to the Christians in Thessalonica (1 Thessalonians 4:14-17).

When Jesus returns for the Christians who are still alive on the earth, Paul says He will bring with Him those Christians who died earlier. This comment can mean only one thing. When Christians die, they go to heaven immediately.

But Christians do not stay in heaven forever. When Christ returns, He will establish a kingdom on earth, a kingdom that will last for one thousand years (Revelation 20:4). If, as Paul said, *"we shall always be with the Lord"* when He returns, it makes sense that we will be included in this kingdom. Keep in mind, this is an earthly kingdom (Revelation 20:4-5). So once again, believers will make their home on earth.

When the thousand years are completed, and Satan has been defeated once and for all (Revelation 20:7-10), God will re-create the earth. God will not only re-create the earth; He is planning to move in! Instead of people dying and going to heaven, John presents us with a picture of God packing up and coming to earth. The point is, after Christ returns, we are back on earth forever. Sin and death will be destroyed, thus erasing any potential division between us and our Creator. All in all, God's original plan will be fulfilled.

What does all this have to do with eternal security? A great deal. First, it answers the question where believers will be eternally secure. Second, it throws a theological monkey wrench into the notion that if we get to heaven, that is all that matters. This is not all that matters because heaven is just a stopover. Heaven is temporary. We are all coming back one way or another.

The bliss of heaven ought not to be thought of simply as intensification of the pleasures of this life. Eternity is not a huge white room where we will all wander around looking for interesting historical figures to chat with. It is not going to be one long church service. Neither will it be one continual game of golf, or softball, or whatever else we enjoy doing. We will not be wearing white robes and walking around on clouds. It is not many of the things we have imagined, for we who are believers will spend eternity on earth.

So, the question remains, will what we do then have anything to do with what we are doing now?

WILL WHAT WE DO THEN HAVE ANYTHING TO DO WITH WHAT WE ARE DOING NOW?

"Now if anyone builds on this foundation with gold, silver, precious stones, wood, hay, straw, each one's work will become clear; for the Day will declare it, because it will be revealed by fire; and the fire will test each one's work, of what sort it is" (1 Corinthians 3:12, 13)

This statement is one of the strongest supporting eternal security to be found in the entire Bible. In this passage the apostle Paul relates what will happen at the Judgement Seat of Christ. Every believer's life will be evaluated on his or her contribution and commitment to the kingdom of God, of which Christ is pictured as the foundation.

Two kinds of Christians are portrayed here. The first one who steps up to be evaluated represents those who have made real contributions to God's kingdom during their earthly lives. Their works are described as "gold, silver, precious stones." They are of such quality that they survive the intense examination of the Savior. Consequently, this person is rewarded for their faithfulness.

Then the second one steps up. They represent believers who have no time for the things of Christ, who live their lives for themselves. One by one their deeds are evaluated, and one by one they burn. Their works are described as "wood, hay, straw." Their works have no real substance, no eternal value.

When the smoke clears, they are faced with the reality that in God's estimation, nothing they have live for has counted. They have spent their entire life pursuing things. Their earthly success has focused on those things that are perishable, temporary. Paul says this person will suffer loss. That is, they will have nothing to show for their life; they will have lost everything. But, Paul concludes, the person themselves will be saved!

This passage is so powerful because we are presented with a Christian who at no point in their entire life bore any eternal fruit. And yet their salvation is never jeopardized. There is never a question about where they will spend eternity.

Despite their secure position as a child of God, this individual probably did not leave the scene rejoicing. Their entire life was written off as a heap of smoldering kindling. And to make things even worse, their Savior, to whom they owed everything, acted as their Judge. This person truly suffered loss.

And it did not end there. For Scripture tells us that a person's faithfulness or unfaithfulness in this life results in a great deal more than simply a moment of rejoicing or shame at the Judgement Seat of Christ. What takes place at the judgement seat has enduring consequences.

A BIBLICAL ILLUSTRATION.

The Gospels are full of parables illustrating this very point. One such parable focuses on a landowner who entrusted his possessions to three slaves while he was gone on a journey (Matthew 25:14-30). He gave each slave a different amount to care for, an amount warranted by individual ability.

The first two slaves invested their master's possessions and doubled their investments. The third slave, however, buried his master's talents in the ground.

The two slaves had been entrusted with different amounts. Yet they both received the same reward. From this outcome, we gain insight into God's standard for judgement. Each of us will be judged based on individual opportunities and abilities (vs. 15). This fact is underscored by the master's reaction to the third slave. He had done nothing with his master's talent. He had not even tried to do anything with it.

At that point in the parable Jesus detoured to make a comment. He knew his listeners would wonder why the slave with ten talents was given one more. One would think the slave with four would have received it. But that is not the way things will be done in His kingdom. *"For to everyone who has, more will be given, and he will have abundance; but from him who does not have, even what he has will be taken away"* (Matthew 25:29). It was Jesus' way of illustrating what happened to the man who came to the judgement seat with wood, hay, and straw. When the judgement was over, even that was taken away.

Christ's meaning is clear. Those who demonstrate in this life an ability and willingness to properly use and invest what God has entrusted to them will be given more to use and invest in His future kingdom. The first two slaves were faithful with a few things. Their reward was the opportunity to be faithful with even more.

The final verse of this parable is so severe that many commentators assume it is a description of hell. It is not. Keep in mind that this is a parable. A parable is used to make one central point. The point of this parable is that in God's future kingdom, those who were faithful in this life will be rewarded and those who were not will lose any potential reward. Some will be given more privileges and responsibility while others will have none.

Here is the verse. *"And cast the unprofitable servant into the outer darkness. There will be weeping and gnashing of teeth."* (Matthew 25:30)

Before we can understand the full impact of the parable we must first determine what the "outer darkness" refers to in the context of the parable. It certainly does not mean hell in the parable. How could a master throw a slave into hell?

To be in the "outer darkness" is to be in the kingdom of God but outside the circle of men and women whose faithfulness on this earth earned them a special rank or position of authority. The "outer darkness" represents not so much an actual place as it does a sphere of influence and privilege. It is not a geographical area in the kingdom where certain men and women are consigned to stay. It is simply a figure of speech describing their low rank or status in God's kingdom.

Imagine standing before God and seeing all you have lived for reduced to ashes. How do you think you would feel? How do you think you would respond? Picture yourself watching saint after saint rewarded for faithfulness and service to the King and all the time knowing that you had just as many opportunities but did nothing about them.

We cannot conceive of the agony and frustration we would feel if we were to undergo such an ordeal; the realization that our faithfulness had cost us eternally would be devastating. And so, it will be for many believers.

We do not know how long this time of rejoicing and sorrow will last. Those whose works are burned will not weep and gnash their teeth for eternity. At some point, we know God will comfort those who have suffered loss (Revelation 21:4). But there is no indication from Scripture that everyone will share the same privileges for eternity. The rewards are permanent.

****

The kingdom of God will not be the same for all believers. Let me put it another way.

- Some believers will have rewards for their earthly faithfulness; others will not.
- Some believers will be entrusted with certain privileges; others will not.
- Some will reign with Christ; others will not (2 Timothy 2:12).
- Some will be rich in the kingdom of God; others will be poor (Luke 12:21, 33).
- Some will be given true riches; others will not (Luke 16:11).
- Some will be given heavenly treasures of their own; others will not (Luke 16:12).
- Some will reign and rule with Christ; others will not (Revelation 3:21).

Privilege in the kingdom of God is determined by one's faithfulness in this life. This truth may come as a shock. Maybe you have always thought that everyone would be equal in the kingdom of God. It is true that there will be equality in terms of our inclusion in the kingdom of God but not in our rank and privilege.

No deeds go unnoticed. All of us must give account. No one gets by with anything. If you are a believer living for Christ, this news should be encouraging. If, however, you are one of those believers who has been content just to know you are on your way to heaven, this information should be disturbing.

REFLECTIONS AND MEDITATIONS

1. Our spiritual state in heaven, regarding our earthly deeds, is just as important as getting there.

CHAPTER 13

"CROWNS: ETERNAL REWARDS"

"and when the Chief Shepherd appears, you will receive the crown of glory that does not fade away."
(1 Peter 5:4)

A crown is special headgear used to symbolize a person's high status, authority, or royalty. What does the bible say, if anything, about the matter of crowns?

When we think about heaven and what we will receive there, we are well reminded of eternal life, streets paved with gold, trees for the healing of the nations, and a mansion of some sort that Jesus has prepared for us. These are all declared to be there for us. However, we need to recognize that there are not only those things but also rewards that have been promised and are available to us based on our earthly commitment, faith, service, etc. while here on earth. God does not want us saved just to escape hell, but to live a full life for Jesus and receive eternal rewards that he has prepared for those that love Him. The crowns we wear in heaven must all be won on earth.

Heaven is not something that we work to attain it is a gift that God freely gives His children. There is equality in Heaven on the basis that no one is there on their own merit. In Heaven, no one will boast that they are there because they deserve to be. Heaven is the result of our faith in the redeeming work of Jesus

Christ. Heaven is based on our acceptance of the fact that Jesus paid the penalty for our sins on the cross of Calvary. Our sins merit eternal Hell but because of the precious blood of Jesus Christ, we are washed white as snow. Perhaps the most correct view of Heaven would be to see it as an inheritance. Inherit means to come into possession of or receive especially as a right or divine portion. An inheritance is something of value that is given to children who are rightful heirs. We do not earn an inheritance it is freely given to those who are heirs. Through what Christ has done for us we are adopted as children into God's family and made heirs of His Kingdom. So, the bottom line is that Heaven is not a reward but it will be a place of rewards.

The Bible talks about five different crowns that are rewards to the faithful Christian; five crowns of eternal rewards.

CROWN OF LIFE

"Blessed is the man who endures temptation; for when he has been approved, he will receive the crown of life which the Lord has promised to those who love Him." (James 1:12)

"Do not fear any of those things which you are about to suffer. Indeed, the devil is about to throw some of you into prison, that you may be tested, and you will have tribulation ten days. Be faithful until death, and I will give you the crown of life." (Revelation 2:10)

Bill Broadhurst was a great runner and he entered a 10K race in Omaha, a race that Bill Rodgers would win in less than 30 minutes. Bill Broadhurst had a handicap, he was paralyzed on his entire left side from an aneurism early in life. But he still loved to run and for him to be in the same race as his hero Bill Rodgers was the greatest thing he could imagine. The banners had been taken down, the traffic had begun to flow on the roads, there was nothing left that would tell you that a race had been run. Except one man Bill Broadhurst who was still running the race. Two hours ago, Bill Rodgers had finished the race and now Bill Broadhurst was nearing the place where the finish line was. A couple of kids on bikes road beside him and said, "Hey mister are you still running the race, it's been over for hours, someone's already finished first and won, why don't you quit, the race is over!" Broadhurst replied, "I can't, I have to make it to my hero at the end of the line." And he kept on running. As he approached the place where he knew the finish line would be, Bill Rodgers and about 30 people stepped out from an alley and they placed a banner up and strung a ribbon across the road. And Bill Broadhurst stumbled across the finish line. And there stood his hero, Bill Rodgers who took off the ribbon from his neck and placed it around the neck of Broadhurst, and he said, "You a winner because you never quit". My fellow believers, don't quit, keep running. Your hero Jesus Christ is at the finish line waiting to give YOU the victor's crown of life. Today, if you are not a Christian, you need to join the only race that will give you a victor's prize. And we Christians need to keep running the race. Jesus is at the finish line waiting for you. He wants to place the golden crown of life on your head.[80]

We all have some handicaps; all of us have a limp. The crown of life is promised to the spiritually mature, to all those who through trial, tribulation, hardships, and handicaps endure to the end. The winner in a race most often is the one who has trained the hardest and disciplined himself the best (1 Corinthians 9:24).[81] Charles Haddon Spurgeon 1834-1892) said, "There are no crown wearers in heaven who were not cross bearers here below."

This crown is promised to those who love God and devote themselves to Him in every area of their lives. It is not just a 'ho hum' love. It is a love that is completely devoted to God. It is the type of love that loves the Lord more than our own lives. The scripture says to love the Lord your God with all your mind, heart, soul, and strength. It is the type of love that will cause us to take up our cross and follow Him, and cause us to set aside everything and everyone so that God can be glorified in us. The crown of life, or the lover's crown as it is sometimes called, is given to the believer who loves the Lord more than his own life. The crown of life is promised to all who have the love of God reigning in their hearts

Every soul that truly loves God shall have its trials in this world fully rewarded in that world above, where love is made perfect. The tried Christian shall be a crowned one, and the crown he shall wear will be a crown of life. We only bear the cross for a while, but we shall wear the crown to eternity.

AN IMPERISHABLE CROWN
(CROWN OF SELF-DENIAL)

"And everyone who competes for the prize is temperate in all things. Now they do it to obtain a perishable crown, but we for an imperishable crown."
(1 Corinthians 9:25)

Paul uses the athletic efforts of the Greeks and Romans to illustrate the intensity with which we should discipline ourselves for Christian activities. The crown was a symbol of victory and reward in the Grecian games. These crowns—circlets, either of green herbs or of pine—were usually made of leaves that soon began to wither. In opposition to these is the imperishable, or incorruptible crown of the Christian. This crown is for competitors not spectators—for *"everyone who competes."* This crown is not for people in the stands but those on the track.

Often, we use the expression "get serious." In basketball, baseball, or football, all kidding or fooling around" is held down when the big game is near. The coach says, "Let's get serious." We may live through a period when eating is a wild delight and a frenzy of calorie-disregarding adventure. But one day we look in astonishment at the numbers on a scale, and say, "I must get serious about losing weight." The apostle is urging us to regard our Christian life with a sense of its supreme significance. We are living in a world where there is real sin. People are hurt, humiliated, and harassed. There is a real death to be faced and an endless eternity to be entered. It is indeed important to get serious about our way and our work in Christ.[82]

In 1 Corinthians 9:26-27 Paul declares of his personal discipline, *"Therefore I run thus: not with uncertainty. Thus I fight: not as one who beats the air. But I discipline my body and bring it into subjection, lest, when I have preached to others, I myself should become disqualified."*

The Incorruptible Crown is for those who take the Christian life seriously and discipline the other areas of life to ensure they do not become disqualified.

CROWN OF REJOICING (or, SOUL WINNERS CROWN)

For what is our hope, or joy, or crown of rejoicing?
Is it not even you in the presence of our Lord Jesus
Christ at His coming? (1 Thessalonians 2:19)

The Roman emperor Charlemagne has an interesting story surrounding his burial. This famous king asked to be entombed sitting upright in his throne. He asked that his crown be placed on his head and his scepter in his hand. He requested that the royal cape be draped around his shoulders and an open book be placed in his lap. That was A.D. 814. Nearly two hundred years later, Emperor Othello determined to see if the burial request had been carried out. He allegedly sent a team of men to open the tomb and make a report. They found the body just as Charlemagne had requested. Only now, nearly two centuries later, the scene was gruesome. The crown was tilted, the mantle moth-eaten, the body disfigured. But open on the skeletal thighs was the book Charlemagne had requested – the Bible. One bony finger pointed to Matthew 16:26, *"What good will it be for a man if he gains the whole world, yet forfeits his soul?"*[83]

There is no greater joy then leading someone to the Lord. The degree of your joy in heaven will be determined by the souls you have had a part in bringing to Christ. In this scripture, Paul is saying that the Thessalonians, are his hope, or joy and crown of rejoicing.

We know that the bible says that when one person comes to know God there is great rejoicing in heaven (Luke 15:10). One day we will, when we receive that crown of rejoicing, be among those who rejoice in heaven. If you have ever directed someone to the Lord you have experienced some of that joy already, but it pales in comparison to the joy that will be known and felt in heaven.

John 4:36 says that we will join with others who have worked to bring others to the Lord, *"And he that reaps receives wages, and gathers fruit unto life eternal: That both he that sows and he that reaps may rejoice together."* We will celebrate with the sower, the reaper, and the person who has come to know the Lord. There will be people celebrating with us because they sowed into our lives, we will be celebrating with others we have sown into and so on.[84]

Therefore, to receive this crown:

- We must live that others may see Christ in us.
- We must give so that others may know Christ.
- We must speak that others may know of Christ and His great love for them.

Whatever you do don't miss out on receiving the crown of rejoicing. It is for those who direct others to Christ. [85]

CROWN OF RIGHTEOUSNESS

In 2 Timothy 4:7, 8, Paul stresses the importance of faithfulness to the end: *"I have fought the good fight, I have finished the race, I have kept the faith. Finally, there is laid up for me the crown of righteousness, which the Lord, the righteous Judge, will give to me on that Day, and not to me only but also to all who have loved His appearing."* Being a Christian is not some light commitment that may be kept for a time and then laid aside when it becomes heavy or inconsistent. One does not enlist in the Lord's army for six months or a year, but for the duration of one's life or until the Lord returns.[86]

The crown of believers is a crown of righteousness, purchased by the righteousness of Christ, and bestowed as the reward of the saints' righteousness.

This crown, which believers shall wear, is laid up for them; meaning that we do not have it not at present, but it is our inheritance that we will receive *"on that day"* (a reference to Christ's return, not Paul's death), side by side with the rest of the faithful who have longed for His appearing. (Philippians 3:20-21; Titus 2:13).[87]

God will give it as *a righteous Judge.* He will give it to all who love, prepare, and long for His appearing. The Crown of Righteousness is for those who lived by determined faith, lived full, and died empty. They have given their all. When the final siren sounds, there is no what if's, could have's, regrets. They are total spent. This reward is for those who have . . .

- Poured out their lives as an offering to God. They have given their whole lives in service for the Lord.
- Fought the good fight.
- Finished the race.

This reward is for completers. It is amazing how many people with faith start but have not finished stuff in their life. They start well and run for a while but then there is always a reason for not crossing the finish line.

TD Jakes once said as he was preaching, "I'm not interested in your praise when God comes through for you. I'm interested in your praise when He doesn't. When the person doesn't get healed, the finance doesn't come through, when people don't like what you did and said, when you lose your job, can't pay the rent. Faith is praising God like Paul and Silas when you're still in the prison."[88]

CROWN OF GLORY (CROWN OF THE UNDERSHEPHERD, or the Pastor's Crown)

"And when the Chief Shepherd appears, you will receive the crown of glory that does not fade away."
(1 Peter 5:4)

In the game follow-the-leader, there is ultimately one leader, the one whom all the other leaders follow. Peter reminds his readers that there is a Chief Shepherd, Jesus Himself, the true leader, the pioneer of the journey of our faith. The Chief Shepherd thus is the ultimate leader and the ultimate example of leadership. He has gone on before us and is waiting to give something to faithful leaders when they reach the end of their journey. It is a crown—a glorious crown because it shares His glory, an unfading crown because it partakes of eternity.[89]

Christian leaders who faithfully guide and guard the Lord's flock will be given a crown, not because they share Christ's reign but because they share His victory.[90]

The Crown of Glory is often referred to as the Pastor's Crown, given to pastor's who . . .

- Serve willingly not by compulsion.
- Serve eagerly and not just for money.
- Love and do not lord it over the people.

Matthew 10:40-42 declares, *"He who receives you receives Me, and he who receives Me receives Him who sent Me. "He who receives a prophet in the name of a prophet shall receive a prophet's reward. And he who receives a righteous man in the name of a righteous man shall receive a righteous man's reward. "And whoever gives one of these little ones only a cup of cold water in the name of a disciple, assuredly, I say to you, he shall by no means lose his reward."* The reward that God gives to pastors and righteous people; the blessings conferred upon them shall pass also upon their friends. When they give the instructions and comforts of the Word, to those who are kind to the preachers of the Word, then He sends a *prophet's reward*. Prophets' rewards are spiritual blessings in heavenly things, and if we know how to value them, we shall reckon them good payment.

When you honor the man of God, you can receive a reward like theirs. How do you do that?

- God will reward you when you give your pastor a reason to serve joyfully and not with sorrow.
- God will reward you when you generously financially support and meet the needs of your pastor and his ministry. John Bevere in his book "Undercover" wrote – *"If church members take care of their pastors and leaders who serve them, businessmen and other members prosper and are blessed. They enjoy heaven's economy."* That would simply seem to say, that as the head prospers, so prospers the body.
- God will reward you if you follow your pastor's directions, instruction, and example 'as one who speaks for God'.

Members of every church can share in the reward, when their pastor receives his crown of glory.

****

We all want to receive crowns:

1. **THE CROWN OF LIFE** – for those devoted to Jesus.
2. **THE INCORRUPTIBLE CROWN** - for those who lived disciplined lives.
3. **THE CROWN OF REJOICING**- for those who directed people to Jesus.
4. **THE CROWN OF RIGHTEOUSNESS** – for those had determined faith.
5. **THE CROWN OF GLORY** – those who dedicated their life to supporting God's leaders.

Crowns have always been the sign of authority and Kingship. **Charlemagne**, whom historians say should deserve to be called "great" above all others, wore an octagonal crown. Each of the eight sides was a plaque of gold, and each plaque was studded with emeralds, sapphires, and pearls. The cost was the price of a king's ransom. **Richard the Lion Heart** had a crown so heavy that two earls had to stand, one on either side, to hold his head. The crown that **Queen Elizabeth** wears is worth over $20 million. **Edward II** once owned nine crowns, something of a record. Put them all together, from all of Europe and from the archives of the East, all of them are but trinkets compared to Christ's crown. Revelation 19 says He has many diadems. He wears a crown of righteousness. He wears a crown of glory. He wears a crown of life. He wears a crown of peace and power. Among those crowns, one outshines the rest. It was not formed by the skilled fingers of a silversmith, nor created by the genius of a craftsman. It was put together hurriedly by the rough hands of Roman soldiers. It was not placed upon its wearer's head in pomp and ceremony, but in the hollow mockery of ridicule and blasphemy. It is a crown of thorns. The amazing thing is that it belonged to me and you. We deserved to wear that crown. We deserved to feel the thrust of the thorns. We deserved to feel the warm trickle of blood upon our brow. We deserved the pain. He took our crown of thorns--but without compensation. He offers to us instead His crown of life, the crown that fadeth not away.

- He wrestled with justice, that we might have rest.
- He wept and mourned, that we might laugh and rejoice.
- He was betrayed, that we might go free.
- He was apprehended, that we might escape.
- He was condemned, that we might be justified.
- He was killed, that we might live.
- He wore a crown of thorns, that we might wear a crown of glory.
- He was nailed to the cross with His arms wide open, that we might wear a crown of life.

William Golson Jr.

We don't want our lives to be a waste, we don't want to just scrape into heaven. But we want to live full and die empty Let us surrender ourselves afresh to Him today. Give Him our lives again as living sacrifices, holy and pleasing to Him. Therefore, we can stand before God on that great day—unashamed and receive our crowns.

REFLECTIONS AND MEDITATIONS

1. If you were to die today, which crown(s) do you hope or think you will have won?

ENDNOTES

1 Winfried Corduan, *No Doubt About It: The Case for Christianity*, (Nashville: Broadman-Holman, 1997), 38
2 R. Laird Harris, *Exploring the Basics of the Bible*, (Wheaton: Crossway Books, 2002), 14
3 Harris, 13
4 "What Christians Think About the Bible", Thomas Peck http://www.sermoncentral.com/sermons/what-christians-think-about-the-bible-timothy-peck-sermon-on-apologetics-the-bible 33127.asp?page=0
5 "How Do I Know the Bible is True?", Dave McFadden http://www.sermoncentral.com/sermons/how-do-i-know-the-bible-is-true-dave-mcfadden-sermon-on-apologetics-the-bible-73032.asp
6 The Open Bible, KJV, Christian Life Study Notes-Master Outline Number One, 2 Peter 1:21, 1167
7 Harris, 37
8 Bible Illustrator, Topic: Bible, SubBible Illustrator, Topic:, Index: 414-434, Date:, Title: Let the Word of God do its Work!
9 Robert J. Morgan, Evidence and Truth, (Wheaton: Crossway Books, 2003), 7
10 Ibid., 80
11 "How Do I Know the Bible is True?", Dave McFadden
12 "Is the Bible Reliable", Joseph Rodgers, http://www.sermoncentral.com/sermons/is-the-bible-reliable-joseph-rodgers-sermon-on-apologetics-the-bible-89382.asp
13 Harris, 62
14 "How Do I Know the Bible is True?", Dave McFadden
15 Is the Bible Reliable, Joseph Rodgers

16 "CSI Jerusalem - Eyewitness Testimony", Jeff Strite http://www. sermoncentral.com/sermons/csi-jerusalem--eyewitness-testimony-jeff-strite-sermon-on-easter-resurrection-91077.asp

17 Morgan, 12

18 Is the Bible Reliable, Joseph Rodgers

19 Ibid.

20 Evidence and Truth, 59

21 Morgan, 9

22 Ibid., 86

23 How You Can Know the Bible is the Word of God, pt. 2, Jerry Shirley http://www.sermoncentral.com/sermons/how-you-can-know-the-bible-is-the-word-of-god-pt-2-jerry-shirley-sermon-on-apologetics-the-bible-68481.asp

24 Origins #1: CREATION, Chris Jordan, http://www.sermoncentral. com/sermons/origins-1-creation-chris-jordan-sermon-on-creation-151629.asp

25 Evolution vs. Creation: The Great Debate, Randy Croft, http://www. sermoncentral.com/sermons/evolution-vs-creation-the-great-debate-randy-croft-sermon-on-evolution-38666.asp

26 Bible Illustrator, Topic: Creator, SubBible Illustrator, Topic:, Index: 884-886, Date: 3/1989.10, Title:

27 Bible Illustrator, Topic: Creator, SubBible Illustrator, Topic:, Index: 884-886, Date: 3/1986.24, Title: Who Can Fix Us?

28 Erickson, 153

29 109

30 "Does God Exist? Is there evidence for the existence of God?" (n.d.). Retrieved [October 21, 2016], from https://gotquestions.org/Does-God-exist.html.

31 Ibid.

32 God Really Exists. Really!, Jeff Strite, http://www.sermoncentral.com/ sermons/god-really-exists-really-jeff-strite-sermon-on-apologetics-god-139097.asp

33 "Does God Exist? Is there evidence for the existence of God?" (n.d.). Retrieved [October 21, 2016], from https://gotquestions.org/Does-God-exist.html.

34 "Does God Exist? Is there evidence for the existence of God?" (n.d.). Retrieved [October 21, 2016], from https://gotquestions.org/Does-God-exist.html.

35 Ibid.

36 "Is there an argument for the existence of God?" (n.d.). Retrieved [October 21, 2016], from https://gotquestions.org/argument-existence-God.html

37 Ibid.

38 "Does God Exist? Is there evidence for the existence of God?"

39 Blaise Pascal, "The Wager," in *The Wager and Other Selections from the Pensees* (Virginia: The Trinity Forum, 1995), 32.

40 "What is Pascal's Wager?" (n.d.). Retrieved [October 21, 2016], from https://gotquestions.org/Pascals-wager.html.

41 Ibid.

42 Pascal, 32.

43 Ibid.

44 Ibid.

45 Ibid., 34.

46 Ibid., 32.

47 Ibid.

48 Ibid.

49 Ibid., 33.

50 Ibid.

51 Ibid.

52 Ibid.

53 Ibid., 34.

54 Ibid.

55 Ibid.

56 The Reward Factor, Denn Guptill, http://www.sermoncentral.com/sermons/the-reward-factor-denn-guptill-sermon-on-sermon-on-the-mount-40349.asp

57 Ibid.

58 Just Have Faith, Timothy Proctor Sr. D. Min, http://www.sermoncentral.com/sermons/just-have-faith-timothy-proctor-sr-d-min-sermon-on-faith-general-52661.asp

59 Ibid.

60 "Who Is Jesus Christ?" (n.d.). Retrieved [October 21, 2016], from https://gotquestions.org/who-is-Jesus.html

61 "What does it mean that Jesus is the Son of Man?" (n.d.). Retrieved [October 21, 2016], from https://gotquestions.org/Jesus-Son-of-Man.html

62 Ibid.

63 Da Vinci Code: Will the Real Jesus Please Stand Up?, Brian Bill, http://www.sermoncentral.com/sermons/da-vinci-code-will-the-real-jesus-please-stand-up-brian-bill-sermon-on-false-teaching-90697.asp

64 Ibid.

65 John F Walvoord and Roy B Zuck, *The Bible Knowledge Commentary: New Testament,* (Wheaton: Victor Books, 1983), 57

66 Da Vinci Code: Will the Real Jesus Please Stand Up?, Brian Bill

67 Got Questions, Does the Bible Record the Death of the Apostles?

68 Dying for the Cause, Jerry Shirley, http://www.sermoncentral.com/sermons/dying-for-the-cause-jerry-shirley-sermon-on-persecution-134734.asp

69 Ibid.

70 Ibid.

71 Ibid.

72 Ibid.

73 Ibid.

74 Ibid.

75 Ibid.

76 Ibid.

77 Jim Cymbala, Fresh Power, (Grand Rapids: Zondervan, 2003), 123

78 Bible Illustrator, Topic: Holy Spirit, SubBible Illustrator, Topic: Dwells in Believers, Index: 1602, Date: 3/1986.26, Title: Vacuum or Victory

79 Bible Illustrator, Topic: Accountability, SubBible Illustrator, Topic: Index: 3452, Date: 6/1998.1004, Title: When a Promise Is Broken

80 *Let's Go For The Gold!* Contributed by: Steve Malone

81 *Standard Lesson Commentary,* (Standard Publishing: Colorado Springs 1995-1996), 348

82 *Standard Lesson Commentary,* (Standard Publishing: Colorado Springs 1994-1995), 310

83 *Encyclopedia of 7700 Illustrations* (Rockville, MD: Assurance Publishers, 1979) Contributed by: David Yarbrough

84 *Crowns of Eternal Reward*, David Becker, http://www.sermoncentral. com/sermons/crowns-of-eternal-reward-david-becker-sermon-on-second-coming-90751.asp?page=0

85 Ibid.

86 *Standard Lesson Commentary*, 1995-1996, 348

87 *The Bible Knowledge Commentary*, NT, 758

88 *Crowns of eternal reward*, David Becker

89 *Standard Lesson Commentary*, (Standard Publishing: Colorado Springs 1991-1992), 307

90 Ibid.

BIBLIOGRAPHY

Bible Illustrator, Parson Technology Inc., bible-illustrator. softwareinformer.com

Courdan, Wifried, *No Doubt About It: The Case for Christianity*, Nashville: Broadman-Holman, 1997

Cymbala, Jim, *Fresh Power*, Grand Rapids: Zondervan, 2003

Erickson, Millard, *Christian Theology, Grand Rapids*, Baker Books House Company, 1985

Encyclopedia of 7700 Illustrations, Rockville, MD: Assurance Publishers, 1979

Evans, William, *The Great Doctrines of the Bible*, Chicago: Moody Press, 1992

Harris, R. Laird, *Exploring the Basics of the Bible*, Wheaton: Crossway Books, 2002

Kinnaman, David, *You Lost Me*, Grand Rapids: Baker Books, 2011

Morgan, Robert J, *Evidence and Truth*, Wheaton: Crossway Books, 2003

Pascal, Blaise, *The Wager," In the Wager and Other Selections from the Pensees* Virginia: The Trinity Forum, 1995

Standard Lesson Commentary, Colorado Springs: Standard Publishing, 1991-1996

The Open Bible, KJV, Christian Life Study Notes

Walvoord, John F and Zuck, Roy B, *The Bible Knowledge Commentary, New Testament,* Wheaton: Victor Books, 1983